Welcome to

Alabama

the *Beautiful*

Alabama
BACK ROAD RESTAURANT
Recipes

A Cookbook &
Restaurant Guide

ANITA MUSGROVE

Great American Publishers
www.GreatAmericanPublishers.com
TOLL-FREE 1-888-854-5954

Great American Publishers

171 Lone Pine Church Road • Lena, MS 39094
TOLL-FREE 1-888-854-5954 • www.GreatAmericanPublishers.com

ISBN 978-1-934817-13-1

10 9 8 7 6

by Anita Musgrove

Layout and design by Cyndi Clark

All images are copyrighted by the creator noted through thinkstock/istock/ (unless otherwise indicated).

Front cover: scenic drive in Mentone, istock/toddmedia • barbecue, bhofack2 • cafe eat sign, istock/creatista • **Back cover:** guest check ticket, devonyu • Alabama quarter, thinkstock/stock/nieuwenhuis • coffee, thinkstock/stock/karandaev • stained napkin, thinkstock/stock/nastco • starfish, thinkstock/hemera/antonio ovejero dfaz • car keys, ferliachirull • open sign, mumble • salt and pepper shakers, hannahgleg • bottle cap, lucato • red checked napkin, ajafoto • red plastic fork, kathleen melis • GPS, thinkstock/hemera/yangyu • **Pages 1–3:** welcome to Alabama sign, wellesenterprises • star cookie cutter, claudio baldini • Cherokee Ridge, Shackleford-PhotographyCollection • sunglasses, thinkstock/photoobjects/gettyimages • condiments tray, sebalos • open sign, mumble • tictac game, thinkstock/hemerorelease/zeljkobozic • car keys, ferliachirulli • **Pages 7–9:** polaroid, istock/Nic_Taylor • cotton, thinkstock/stock • pickled vegetables, chrisevans • eat sign, trekandshoot • best hot dogs stamp, roxanabalint • hot dog, thinkstock/photoobjects/gettyimages • **Page 11:** sky, karandaev • coffee, thinkstock/stock/karandaev • gas price sign, thinkstock/stock/paulhart • volkswagen van, thinkstock/stock/robingeorge • telescope, trekandshoot • stained napkin, thinkstock/stock/nastco • Alabama quarter, thinkstock/stock/nieuwenhuis • rocket, thinkstock/fuse • blue star, natalia • moped, risteski • **Page 13:** camo hat, taviphoto • blueberry jam, inganeilsen, open sign, mumble • **Page 25:** U.S. Space & Rocket Center, Carol M. Highsmith • monkey, Byrdyak • **Page 39:** pine cone, dianataliun • green leaf, thinkstock/photos.com/gettyimages • maple leaf, gansovskyViadislav • rabbit, GlobalP • deer crossing, Harris Shiffman • daisies, thinkstock/Stockbyte/Brand X • **Page 51:** chapel photos used by permission of Reverend Ron Reynolds • crucifix: gettyimages • **Page 57:** Headphones, snowflock • records, stuckpixels • cassette, filipfoto • sheet music, mark wragg • guitar, petr malyshev • microphone, thinkstock • **Pages 70–71:** stamp, alexanderzam • toy race car, paul beverley • checkered flag, viktor blazhuk • salt and pepper shakers, hannahgleg • bottle cap, lucato • heart crackers, garsya • red plastic fork, kathleen melis • red checked napkin, ajafoto • star earrings, thinkstock/zoonar • neon eat sign, trekandshoot • **Page 93:** Peaches, valentyn volkov • **Page 111:** Noccalula Falls, wikipedia.org/thejammer • **Pages 128–129:** leaves, silverjohn • toast, akiyoko • guest check ticket, devonyu • pine cone, dianataliun • toy camper truck, thinkstock/photoobjects.net/gettyimages • gas nozzle, thinkstock/stock • condiments tray, sebalos • GPS, thinkstock/hemera/yangyu • sweet home sign, nataliaBratslavsky • largemouth bass, willard • **Page 131:** dogwood trees: wendellandCarolyn • blossom: melindaFawver • **Page 141:** peanuts, valery121283 • **Page 162:** car, on display at Hank Williams Museum, Montgomery • **Page 171:** Sturdivant Hall, Carol M. Highsmith Archive • doll, thinkstock/photoobjects.net/gettyimages • ticker tape machine, jamessteidl • cotton, thinkstock/stock • **Pages 176–177:** sand, nimon_t • starfish, thinkstock/hemera/antonio ovejero dfaz • two sea shells, santje09 • one sea shell, ghettog76 • yellow flipflops, westlight • lemonade, edie layland • arrow sign, thinkstock/photodisc • shrimp basket, danny hooks • sunglasses, thinkstock/photoobjects/gettyimages • yellow napkin, thinkstock/gettyimages/Hemera Technologies • battleship, thinkstock/hemera/dennis gonzales • sailboat, thinkstock/dorling kindersley • **Page 194:** toy train: evangelos kanaridis • **Page 203:** manuscript, imagorb • footprints, ganna rassadnikova • fountain pen, thinkstock/photoobjects.net/gettyimages • **Page 217:** gavel on books, brianajackson • bird, anagramm • Pulitzer prize, PD-1923 • **Page 219:** stamp, William Howell • postcard: Sharon Day • **Page 227:** Dinosaurs, photos courtesy of Barber Marina • **Page 232:** Bellingrath Gardens, The George F. Landegger Collection of Alabama Photographs in Carol M. Highsmith's America, Library of Congress, Prints and Photographs Division.• azaleas: Melinda Fawver • **Pages 240–252:** old suitcase, DrAbbate • white suitcase, thinkstock/PhotoObjects.net/Hemera Technologies • small blue suitcase, Luís Francisco CorderoCollection • chalkboard, uptonpark • soup, IvonneW • napkin set, Michael Flippo • jukebox, agcuesta • neon sign, thinkstock/photodisc/Ryan McVay • milkshakes, thinkstock/gettyimages/Hemera Technologies

Every effort has been made to ensure the accuracy of the information provided in this book.
However, dates, times, and locations are subject to change.
Please call or visit websites for up-to-date information before traveling.

To purchase books in quantity for corporate use, incentives, or fundraising,
please call Great American Publishers at 888-854-5954.

Contents

SWEET DIGS

MOUNTAIN REGION

METROPOLITAN REGION

RIVER REGION

GULF COAST REGION

Preface

Alabama **is truly the Heart of Dixie.** When I hear the word Alabama, my mind goes back in time to my childhood. I was born in Bessemer, and by the age of five, I was living in Healing Springs—one of the smallest bends in the road.

People came from all over the world to drink from the springs, staying either in the world-renowned hotel located there or in cabins converted from ones workers had lived in when the place was a working plantation. Throughout the six years I lived there, I made fast friends with children from all over the world who came with their families to "get healed" at the springs.

The rich iron content that made the springs "healing" was not to be used for every-day drinking. We used bluing in our clothes because the iron-rich water turned everything a nice shade of yellow (orange if the clothing stayed around long enough). I remember hauling drinking water from the artesian well about three miles from our house. I loved to go with Daddy to fill the jugs and get a nice cold drink straight from the well that was always flowing (it still flows to this day).

The Entrance to Healing Springs site which is on private property but open to the public during daylight hours.

Family vacations also meant enjoying time in Alabama. Each year we rented a cottage in Gulf Shores for the whole week of July 4th to enjoy the sugar sand beaches. It was as if I had died and moved to heaven.

We had fun in the sun, ran in the waves, and played in the sand. There was always a fair right down the road from the cottage where you could ride rides until you were so dizzy you had to stand still for a minute or you would fall down and make an idiot of yourself in front of that cute boy who was making eyes at you. In the daytime, there was crabbing on the seawall or deep-sea fishing; at night, cool walks along the shore. Oh, how I enjoyed those Alabama summers.

One summer at home, I thought it would be fun to pick cotton. Luckily, a good friend's father raised cotton. He quickly took us up on our offer to work. Let me tell you, picking cotton is not fun. It only took one row to change our minds, but riding over the hills and hollows in the cotton seed wagon was a lot of fun.

Labor Day week, we would go to Granny Rice and Papaw's summer place in Shelby County to spend the last few days of summer before school started back. We were given the job of pulling peanuts off the vines, because Papaw sold peanuts at the Farmer's Market in Birmingham. He would back his big truck up to the yard, the back full of the vines that were gathered from the fields. We had to pick every peanut before we could race to the red clay river bank and dive in for a cooling swim.

I remember spending many hours helping my Granny shell beans and peas and putting up homemade sauerkraut and beets and tomatoes. The only thing that can compare to dinner at Grandmother's table was a delicious meal out at a local mom-and-pop restaurant.

Many years later, married and living in Mississippi, my husband Leonard and I were notorious for weekend and day-long car trips. We would drive the back roads with no destination in mind other than seeing places we've never been or traveling familiar roads. Nothing is better than jumping in a car in the early morning with no particular place to go, watching the sun come up behind the trees, and just enjoying the beauty that God has created for us.

One of the best things about those trips was stumbling upon a gem of a restaurant that only the locals knew about. We were open for anything—diners, drive-ins,

dives, little hole-in-the-wall places—so long as it was locally owned, but my favorite places in Alabama have always been any place that serves hot dogs. Hot dogs are still my go-to comfort food, and it seems like Alabama is the only place to get a steaming hot dog with sauerkraut.

In this book, it is my goal to capture my love of Alabama, especially her food. I want you to enjoy traveling the back roads as much as I always have and, of course, to have the opportunity to stop in at a locally owned diner for a great meal. To make that easy, I've compiled a list of the favorite places to be found all throughout Alabama. And, because this book is meant for traveling, the restaurants are divided into regions—Mountain, Metropolitan, River, and Gulf Coast. At the beginning of each region, you will find a list of restaurants featured in that section. Throughout each section, the restaurants are presented alphabetically by city. I've told you a little about each one and what makes them special. I hope that you will find time to visit them and see for yourself how great the locally-owned restaurants are in Alabama.

No time to travel? No problem. Each restaurant has shared some of their favorite recipes—it may be a recipe served in the restaurant or a family favorite they serve at home, but every recipe is delicious and presented to make it easy to make at home.

Whether you are driving along the back roads or cooking at home in your kitchen, it is my sincere hope that this book brings you home to Sweet Home Alabama.

Enjoy!

Anita Musgrove

State Back Road Restaurant Cookbook Series

Mountain REGION

11

Hickory Barn Bar-B-Que

12250 U.S. 72
Athens, AL 35611
256-262-4460
www.hickorybarnbbq.com
Traditionalsoutherneatsandbbq.com

Hickory Barn Bar-B-Que is a full-service barbecue restaurant offering on-site catering of everything from whole hog and fish fries to steak dinners. Hickory Barn takes great pride in their barbecue and competes in several cook-offs every year winning Grand Champion at Jack Daniels plus many more awards. They make everything in-house and from scratch including four barbecue sauces, delicious sides, and outstanding desserts. The restaurant is decorated with antique items— old Coke machines, signs, car tags, and dollar bills signed by everyone from Paula Dean to Ted Nugent, senators to country music stars. Ya'll Come!

Thursday: 10:30 am to 8:00 pm
Friday & Saturday:
10:30 am to 9:00 pm
Sunday: 10:30 am to 2:00 pm
Catering and Special Events:
7 days a week

Uncle Booger's Pecan Pie

½ cup softened butter

1 cup sugar

1 cup clear corn syrup

4 eggs, beaten

1 cup chopped pecans

1 teaspoon vanilla extract

1 deep pie shell (or 2 regular pie shells)

Preheat oven to 350°. Combine butter and sugar. Add corn syrup, eggs, pecans and vanilla. Mix well. Pour in pie shell and bake 35 minutes or until set. Let it cool (if you can wait) before you slice and serve. Great served warm with vanilla ice cream!

Restaurant Recipe

LIMESTONE COUNTY COURTHOUSE

Athens, Alabama

Limestone County is in the rolling foothills of the Appalachian Mountains in northern Alabama. Though Limestone County is the smallest county in the state, it has much to offer—from quiet morning walks to beautiful antebellum homes, birds, festivals, art, rodeos, and tractor shows and pulls, to hunting and fishing, horseback riding, cotton picking, shopping, and delicious southern-style cooking.

Go to www.visitathensal.com for more information.

LuVici's Restaurant

105 North Jefferson Street
Athens, AL 35611
256-233-5550
www.luvicis.com

If you are "in the mood for Southern Food," stop in at LuVici's on the square in Athens, connected to the historic U. G. White Mercantile. You'll enjoy a dining experience reminiscent of days gone by, complete with southern etiquette and southern hospitality. The food is the star at this delightful restaurant featuring homestyle breakfast and lunch just like Grandmother made, and upscale Southern dinner choices that include Certified Angus Steaks, Shrimp and Grits, Bayou Skillet Chicken, Mesquite Smoked Ribs, Gorgonzola Butter Shrimp Low Country Crab Cakes and so much more. "Put some South in your mouth" at LuVici's Restaurant.

Monday – Wednesday: 7:00 am to 2:00 pm
Thursday – Saturday: 7:00 am to 8:30 pm

LuVici's Shrimp & Grits

Prepare Gorgonzola Butter and Tomato Cheese Grits in advance.

Gorgonzola Butter:

2 pounds butter, softened

2 tablespoons minced garlic

1 cup panko breadcrumbs

1 cup Parmesan cheese

2 cups Gorgonzola cheese

1 teaspoon black pepper

Combine with electric mixer. Place in container and refrigerate.

Tomato Cheese Grits:

8 cups chicken broth

3 cups diced tomatoes in juice

1 teaspoon salt

2 tablespoons bacon grease

6 cups grits

2 cups chopped bacon or bacon bits

12 slices pepper jack cheese

12 slices Cheddar cheese

Bring broth, tomatoes, salt and bacon grease to boil. Add grits and reduce heat; cook until thickened. Stir in bacon and cheeses until cheese is melted. May be made ahead and refrigerated until use.

Shrimp & Grits:

2½ pounds large (21 to 25 count) shrimp, tail on, peeled and deveined

Cajun seasoning, for garnish

Shredded Parmesan, for garnish

Chopped chives, for garnish

Split each shrimp down the back. In large sauté pan, melt ½ cup Gorgonzola Butter per serving. Add 7 shrimp per serving, and sauté 1 to 2 minutes per side. Place ¾ cup Tomato Cheese Grits per serving in a 6-inch cast iron skillet. Place in preheated 350° oven while cooking shrimp. Stand sautéed shrimp around skillet in the grits with 1 in center, reserve Gorgonzola Butter left in pan. Bake 3 to 4 minutes until shrimp are cooked through but not overcooked. Pour reserved Gorgonzola Butter over shrimp and grits. Sprinkle shrimp with Cajun seasoning, garnish with shredded Parmesan cheese and chopped chives. Serve with a hot baguette.

Restaurant Recipe

THINKSTOCK/ISTOCK/

Parkside Catfish Restaurant

13610 Alabama Highway 69 North
Baileyton, AL 35019
256-796-4288
toll-free 855-238-1418
www.parksidecatfishrestaurant.com

Enjoy the best local, down-home country cooking when you visit Parkside Catfish Restaurant. The magnificent catfish dinners, breakfasts, hamburger steaks, barbecue pork, and so much more offer something for everyone to love. The hushpuppies are super-delicious and the lemon chicken is a local favorite. Friendly service, great atmosphere, and sinfully big portions make Parkside an experience you won't want to miss.

Sunday: 7:00 am to 2:00 pm
Monday – Thursday: 6:00 am to 8:00 pm
Friday & Saturday: 6:00 am to 9:00 pm

Roasted Chicken with New Potatoes

6 (4-ounce) boneless skinless chicken breasts

⅔ cup olive oil

2 teaspoons minced garlic

1 teaspoon dried Italian herbs

1 teaspoon salt

¼ teaspoon black pepper

¼ cup shredded Parmesan cheese

1 pound new red potatoes (small), washed well

Preheat oven to 350°. Treat a 9x13-inch baking dish with nonstick spray. Wash chicken breasts and layer in dish. In a small bowl, combine oil, garlic, herbs, salt and pepper. Lightly coat chicken with mixture—most of it will be reserved for potatoes. Sprinkle cheese over chicken. In a medium bowl, coat potatoes with remaining seasoning mixture. Layer potatoes over and around chicken. Cover and bake 35 to 40 minutes or until chicken is cooked through. Raise oven temperature to 425° and cook, uncovered, another 5 minutes or until chicken breasts are lightly browned. Serves 6.

Local Favorite

Bloody Mary Mix

64 ounces tomato juice

2 tablespoons Dijon mustard

3 tablespoons Worcestershire sauce

2 tablespoons white horseradish

2 tablespoons Crystal hot sauce

2 teaspoons salt

2 tablespoons olive brine (juice)

1 teaspoon celery salt

2 teaspoons black pepper

Juice of 2 limes and 2 lemons

Combine all and refrigerate 2 hours.

Restaurant Recipe

Cranberry Congealed Salad

1 (20-ounce) can crushed pineapple

2 (3-ounce) boxes raspberry Jell-O

3 cups sugar

4 apples, peeled and chopped

4 oranges, peeled and chopped

1 stalk celery, finely chopped

1 (14-ounce) can whole-berry cranberry sauce

2 cups chopped pecans

Heat pineapple, Jell-O and sugar until dissolved. Add remaining ingredients and mix well. Pour into 2 long pans. Serve immediately or refrigerate.

Restaurant Recipe

The All Steak Restaurant

323 Third Avenue Southeast
Cullman, AL 35055
256-734-4322
www.theallsteakrestaurant.com

The All Steak has a long, rich heritage in Cullman. It was first opened in 1934, and those owners wanted to name it "All Steak Hamburgers." Because the sign would have been too expensive, they shortened it to "All Steak." Present owner, Matt Heim, bought the restaurant seven years ago and has developed the new bistro-style building. Specializing in American cuisine, the restaurant offers a wide variety of appetizers and entrées and features a full bar. Their world-famous orange rolls are served daily.

Tuesday – Friday: 10:30 am to 10:00 pm
(lounge closes at midnight

Saturday: 7:30 am to 10:00 pm
(lounge closes at midnight)

Sunday: 7:30 am to 3:00 pm
(buffet open 10:30 am to 2:00 pm)

Busy Bee Café

**101 5th Street Southeast
Cullman, AL 35055
256-734-9958**

Busy Bee Café, established in 1919, serves Cullman and surrounding communities. Famous for their Depression Burgers (also known as Poor Man Burgers), Busy Bee is still serving the original recipe today. Be sure to try their made-from-scratch desserts, too. For breakfast, lunch or dinner, Busy Bee Café is well-known as the place to fill your stomach at a reasonable price.

**Monday – Thursday: 6:00 am to 2:00 pm
Friday & Saturday: 6:00 am to 9:00 pm**

White Chocolate Bread Pudding

½ stick (4 tablespoons) butter

1 loaf French bread, sliced thin or cubed

2 (12-ounce) bags white chocolate chips, divided

3 pints heavy whipping cream, divided

1 cup sugar

3 large eggs

1 teaspoon vanilla extract

Preheat oven to 350°. Melt butter in an 11x13-inch baking dish. Layer bread in dish. Place in oven to lightly toast bread, about 10 minutes. While bread toasts, cook 1 bag chocolate, 2½ pints whipping cream, sugar, eggs and vanilla over medium heat until chocolate is melted and everything is fully incorporated. Pour over toasted bread; bake, uncovered, 45 minutes. Melt remaining bag of chocolate with ½ pint whipping cream; pour over baked bread pudding and serve.

Restaurant Recipe

Peach Crunch Cake

1 (24.5-ounce) can sliced peaches in light syrup, drain and chop peaches into bite-size pieces

1 box yellow cake mix

1 stick (½ cup) butter, cut into 16 equal pieces

1 cup brown sugar

½ cup chopped walnuts

Preheat oven to 350°. Layer ingredients into a 9x13-inch baking dish beginning with peaches. Add each ingredient in the order listed. (Cake mix is just poured on top of peaches straight from box.) Bake 35 to 40 minutes or until bubbly. Serve warm with ice cream or whipped topping. Simple yet delicious.

Family Favorite

Johnny's Bar-B-Q

1401 4th Street SW
Cullman, AL 35055
256-734-8539
www.johnnysbarbq.com

Family owned and operated since 1963, Johnny's Bar-B-Q has been recognized as "Best Of The Best Bar-B-Q In America" by *National Barbecue News*. They have also won the local Readers Choice Award for "Best Bar-B-Q" by the local folks each year since it's origination 16 years ago. Take a taste of their tender pulled pork cooked nightly and you will never eat barbecue anywhere else. Barbecue pork, chicken, and ribs are the stars of the menu. The huge Bar-B-Q Potato is a must try!!!! They also have a varied menu which includes fresh catfish. Kids meals are also offered. Be sure to save room for one of their delicious homemade cheesecakes. Customer service is a top priority.

Tuesday – Saturday: 10:00 am to 9:00 pm

The Old Cookstove Restaurant

89 Reeder Road
Danville, AL 35619
256-462-1151

The Old Cookstove Restaurant, operated by Grandma and Grandpa Yoder, focuses on down-to-earth, old-fashioned food that tastes great. A local favorite is their homemade ice cream. Located on one of the few gravel roads remaining in Morgan County, The Old Cookstove Restaurant is worth the trip. As main cook, you'll find Grandma in the kitchen preparing outstanding dishes. As main talker, Grandpa strolls the dining room visiting with the guests. You may enjoy sitting on the front porch watching squirrels in the yard and birds in the trees, but you will definitely enjoy the hospitality and delicious food.

Thursday: 4:00 pm to 7:00 pm
Friday & Saturday: 11:00 am to 7:00 pm

Chocolate Lovers Dream Cookies

6 tablespoons oil
¼ cup (½ stick) butter, softened
¾ cup packed brown sugar
½ cup sugar
2 eggs
1 teaspoon vanilla extract
1¼ cups all-purpose flour
½ cup baking cocoa
½ teaspoon salt
¼ teaspoon baking powder
1 cup vanilla or white chocolate chips
1 cup milk chocolate chips

Beat oil, butter and both sugars until well blended. Add eggs 1 at a time, beating well after each addition. Beat in vanilla. In a separate bowl, combine flour, cocoa, salt and baking powder. Gradually add to oil mixture and mix well. Stir in chips. Drop by rounded tablespoonfuls onto ungreased baking sheet. Bake at 350° for 10 minutes or until edges begin to brown.

Restaurant Recipe

Sour Cream Potatoes

3 pounds potatoes, peeled and diced

1 small yellow onion, diced

½ cup plus 1 tablespoon butter, divided

2 cups sour cream

¼ cup chives, diced

2½ cups shredded Cheddar cheese, divided

Salt and pepper to taste

Boil potatoes in salted water until tender. While potatoes are cooking, sauté onions in 1 tablespoon butter until soft. Drain potatoes; chunk up the potatoes in the pot by mashing them with your spoon. Add onions, sour cream, chives, 1 cup cheese, and remaining ½ cup butter. Salt and pepper to taste. Transfer to a 9x13-inch casserole dish and cook 45 minutes at 350°. Top with remaining 1½ cups cheese and return to oven just until cheese is melted.

Family Favorite

Libby's Catfish & Diner

1401 Highway 67 South
Decatur, AL 35603
256-353-9767

Libby's Catfish & Diner has been in business since 1996. From day one and every day since, they strive to serve quality food with friendly, efficient service in a home environment. They serve breakfast, home-cooked meals, southern fried catfish, and hand-cut steaks that are cooked to perfection and are so tender they melt in your mouth. Visit Libby's and enjoy the best meals Alabama has to offer—Good Cooking with a Friendly Atmosphere. At Libby's, they always say: "WE HAVE THE BEST CUSTOMERS IN THE WORLD."

Monday – Wednesday:
5:00 am to 8:00 pm
Thursday – Saturday: 5:00 am to 8:30 pm
Sunday: 6:00 am to 3:30 pm

Simp McGhee's

725 Bank Street Northwest
Decatur, AL 35601
256-353-6284
www.simpmcghees.com

Located in the Arts and Entertainment District in historic, downtown Decatur, Simp McGhee's was named after the town's infamous riverboat captain. His boisterous ways, unconventional operations, and blustering manner made him a most picturesque legend of

the Tennessee River. Tales are told of Simp's pet pig that was known to be his drinking partner. Simp McGhee's Restaurant is known for the tales of the Riverboat Captain, his partner Miss Kate, who ran the local brothel and their Cajun/Creole cuisine. Simp McGhee's stuffed mushroom caps are listed in the "100 Dishes to Eat in Alabama Before You Die." Simp McGhee's restaurant features a sidewalk café, upstairs dining with white linen and candlelight, and downstairs features a rustic bar atmosphere.

Monday – Thursday: 5:00 pm to 9:00 pm
Friday & Saturday: 5:00 pm to 9:30 pm

Crystal Shrimp and Grits

Grits:

2 cups heavy cream

2 cups water

1 teaspoon granulated garlic

1 teaspoon granulated onion

1 teaspoon white pepper

1 tablespoon thyme leaves

1 tablespoon kosher table salt

1 cup diced andouille sausage

1 cup stone-ground grits (not instant)

1 cup shredded Parmesan cheese

Bring all ingredients, except grits and cheese, to a boil; add grits. Reduce heat to medium and simmer until done, about 15 minutes. Stir in cheese.

Crystal Sauce:

4 cups fish, chicken or shrimp stock

4 tablespoons blond roux (equal parts fat and flour cooked to a medium to light brown color)

1 each, green, yellow and red bell pepper, small dice

1 medium yellow onion, small dice

3 stalks celery, fine dice

1 teaspoon kosher salt

2 tablespoons Old Bay seasoning

24 jumbo shrimp, peeled and deveined

Slowly whisk stock into hot roux until smooth. Add bell peppers, onion, celery, salt and Old Bay seasoning. Bring to a simmer. Cook 10 minutes; add shrimp and cook 3 minutes more.

In entrée bowl, top prepared grits with shrimp and gravy mixture (6 shrimp per bowl). Recipe serves 4.

Restaurant Recipe

ISTOCK/WSMAHAR

Dutch Oven Bakery

**1205 Evergreen Road
Falkville, AL 35622
256-462-3988**

Dutch Oven Bakery is a great place to find unique, home-style baked goods and candies, or a sandwich (seating outside). The deli uses home-style bread baked on-site to make sandwiches with your choice of meat, cheese, and other goodies. Finish your meal with a slice of home-style pie or cake, also baked on-site. While you are there, be sure to check out their wide variety of "take home goodies." Dutch Oven Bakery is much more than just a bakery. We think you will find the experience enjoyable.

Tuesday – Saturday: 8:30 am to 5:00 pm

Amish Macaroni Salad

2 cups mayonnaise

1 cup water

1 cup Amish Macaroni Salad Mix*

1 (16-ounce) package elbow macaroni

3 to 4 hard-boiled eggs, peeled and chopped

Combine mayonnaise, water and Amish Macaroni Salad Mix; set aside. Cook macaroni in boiling water until tender; cool under cold running water then drain well. Fold macaroni and eggs into dressing. Cover and refrigerate overnight.

Restaurant Recipe

*Amish Macaroni Salad Mix is available at Dutch Oven Bakery. Ready made salad is not sold at the bakery.

SPACE MONKEY GRAVESITE
Huntsville, Alabama

Miss Baker, a squirrel monkey, was one of the first animals to fly in space and return alive. She was sent into space aboard a Jupiter rocket and then brought safely back to earth on May 28, 1959. The flight reached an altitude of 300 miles, while traveling at speeds in excess of 10,000 miles per hour. From 1971 to her death in 1984, she lived at the U.S. Space & Rocket Center, and you will find her gravesite at the entrance to the museum. At the time of her death, at 27 years of age, she was believed to be the oldest squirrel monkey ever documented. While you are at the museum, be sure to visit the U.S. Space & Rocket Center where you will experience the physics of astronaut training like never before in simulators like Space Shot™ and G-Force. Spacedome IMAX Theater transports you to different worlds with amazing documentary films like *Hubble*, and much more.

For more information, go to
www.rocketcenter.com

Cooley's Corner Café

8271 County Road 189 • Florence, AL 35633
256-766-8535 or 256-760-1762

Cooley's Corner Café is a locally-owned old-fashioned café that has served the Florence area for 40 years. When you eat at Cooley's you are treated just like one of the family. They have great food and friendly service. On the weekends, you will love their all-you-can-eat catfish fillets or whole catfish. Cooley's Grocery Store is right next door. Open the same hours as the café except closed Thursdays. Stop by for great food and a fun visit.

Monday – Saturday:
9:00 am to 8:00 pm
Sunday:
11:00 am to 6:00 pm

Lemon Pie

1 (14-ounce) can sweetened condensed milk

1 (12-ounce) can lemonade frozen concentrate

1 (16-ounce) carton Cool Whip

1 graham cracker pie crust

Combine condensed milk and frozen lemonade. Fold in half the Cool Whip. Pour into crust. Top with remaining Cool Whip. Refrigerate until ready to serve.

Family Favorite

Sweet Tooth Dessert

1 (8-ounce) can crushed pineapple (or pineapple chunks), drained

1 (8-ounce) can mandarin oranges, drained

1 (16-ounce) can cherry pie filling

1 (14-ounce) can sweetened condensed milk

1 (12-ounce) carton Cool Whip

Carefully mix first 4 ingredients. Top with Cool Whip. Refrigerate until ready to serve; keep chilled.

Family Favorite

Ham and Cheese Sandwiches

1½ pounds sliced deli ham (4 long slices)

1 (8-ounce) package Swiss cheese (4 long slices)

1 stick butter

2 tablespoons sugar

1 tablespoon grated onion

2 tablespoons poppy seeds

2 tablespoons prepared mustard

Salt and pepper to taste

3 (24-roll) packages ready-to-serve rolls

Cut ham and cheese in small pieces about the size of one roll. Melt butter and mix in remaining ingredients, except rolls. Break rolls in 3 rows. Slice each row open; lay aside. Spread butter mixture on both sides. Top with a slice of cheese and a slice of ham. Fold rolls back together and place back in pan until ready to cook. (Can be made ahead of time and frozen.) Bake fresh rolls 20 minutes at 350°. (If frozen, bake at 250° for 30 minutes.)

Family Favorite

Garden Gate Café

1917 Florence Boulevard
Florence, AL 35360
(256) 349-2569

701 Avalon Avenue
Muscle Shoals, AL 35661
(256) 383-6905

Garden Gate Café should be on your list of "places you must visit" while in the area. You can't beat the quality of the food or the value you get. Not to mention, it has the best country cooking around—authentic southern food straight from granny's kitchen. The food is consistently delicious and the service is quick and friendly. They have a limited menu and a changing meal of the day, but the local favorite is the boneless fried chicken which is tender and juicy. Their selection of desserts will satisfy the sweet tooth. If you are looking for delicious comfort food with heart and soul, Garden Gate Café is the place to go.

Monday – Friday: 10:30 am to 8:00 pm

Apple Toffee Dip

2 (8-ounce) packages cream cheese, softened

¾ cup packed brown sugar

¼ cup sugar

1 teaspoon vanilla extract

1 (8-ounce) package (1½ cups) Heath English Toffee Bits

Using an electric mixer, combine cream cheese and both sugars until mixed well. Add vanilla and toffee bits; mix well. Spoon into a glass serving dish and refrigerate 1 hour or until ready to serve. Serve with cored and quartered red and green apples for dipping.

Local Favorite

THINKSTOCK/ISTOCK

Grandma's Banana Pudding

2 cups sugar, divided

⅔ cup cornstarch

Dash of salt

¾ stick butter or margarine

1½ (12-ounce) cans evaporated milk

18 ounces water
(1½ cans using milk can)

1 tablespoon vanilla extract

9 eggs, separated

1 (12-ounce) box vanilla wafers

4 to 5 bananas

Mix 1½ cups sugar, cornstarch and salt; set aside. Melt butter in double boiler; add milk, water, vanilla and egg yolks. Gradually add sugar mixture, stirring constantly, until it reaches consistency of a thick gravy. Using an electric mixer, beat egg whites medium speed. Gradually add remaining ½ cup sugar, and continue beating until stiff peaks form to make a meringue. Line an 11x13-inch pan with wafers and bananas. Pour filling over top. Spread meringue over pudding. Bake at 350° just until top is lightly browned, about 15 to 20 minutes. Serve warm. Makes approximately 20 servings.

Restaurant Recipe

Singleton's Bar-B-Que

**4220 Huntsville Road
Florence, AL 35630
256-760-0802**

Singleton's Bar-B-Que has been serving the Shoals area since 1957. Aaron Singleton opened the first location in Sheffield and was soon joined by brothers WD and Junior. In 1960, a location was opened in Florence. Rick Singleton, son of Junior, and his wife, Peggy, opened the current location in 1993. Known for their delicious barbecue pork and chicken, Rick and Peggy have expanded the menu to include beef brisket, sausage, and ribs. Some of the unique items you will find on the menu are the "Barnyard Sampler," Pig Trough Taters, and Barburritos. Other staples include Brunswick Stew and delicious homemade pies.

**Tuesday – Thursday: 10:30 am to 8:00 pm
Friday – Saturday: 10:30 am to 9:00 pm
Sunday: 10:30 am to 2:00 pm**

Ol' Tymers BBQ & Blues

2207 Gault Avenue North, Suite J
Fort Payne, AL 35967
256-418-4181

Ol' Tymers BBQ & Blues takes pride in using recipes that have been passed down from generation to generation. They cook their meat low and slow and pack lots of love in each side dish. Delicious homemade recipes fill their menu. Your visit to Ol' Tymers is guaranteed to be an overall great experience as you taste their hard work and dedication in each bite you take. There is also a full bar so you can relax and enjoy the entertainment from various artists.

KITCHEN HOURS:
Thursday – Saturday:
10:00 am to 10:00 pm

BAR HOURS:
Thursday: 10:00 am to 12:00 am
Friday & Saturday: 10:00 am to 2:00 am

A Slice of Orange Cake

1 cup butter, softened

2 cups sugar

4 eggs

1 teaspoon baking soda

½ cup buttermilk

1 cup flaked coconut

3 ½ cups all-purpose flour

1 pound candied orange slices, chopped

2 cups chopped raisins

2 cups chopped nuts

1 cup fresh orange juice

2 cups powdered sugar

1 teaspoon vanilla extract

Cream butter and sugar until smooth. Add eggs 1 at a time, beating well after addition. Dissolve baking soda in buttermilk and add to creamed mixture. Stir in coconut. Place flour in a separate bowl; add orange slices, raisins and nuts, stirring to coat well. Combine the two mixtures into a very stiff dough that should be mixed by hand. Pour into a greased and floured 9x13-inch baking pan. Bake at 250° for 2½ to 3 hours or until tests done. Combine orange juice, powdered sugar and vanilla. Pour over hot cake. Let it sit overnight or up to 2 days before serving.

Local Favorite

Cucumber Salsa

2 cups finely chopped peeled cucumber

½ cup finely chopped peeled tomato

¼ cup chopped red onion

1 jalapeño pepper, seeded and chopped

1 garlic clove, minced

2 tablespoons minced fresh cilantro

¼ cup sour cream

1½ teaspoons lemon juice

1½ teaspoons lime juice

¼ teaspoon ground cumin

¼ teaspoon salt

In a small bowl, combine cucumber, tomato, onion, pepper, garlic and cilantro. In a separate bowl, combine sour cream, lemon juice, lime juice, cumin and salt. Pour over cucumber mixture and toss to coat. Serve immediately with tortilla chips for dipping.

Local Favorite

Barry's Backyard Barbecue

85 County Road 527
Fyffe, AL 35971
256-623-2102

Not your average barbecue restaurant, Barry's Backyard Barbecue is located in the farmer's backyard. The trip is well worth their barbecue which cooks 16 hours using hickory wood and is finished with a splash of Barry's special vinegar-based sauce—a recipe that has taken Barry 16 years to perfect. Folks drive from as far away as Chattanooga and Birmingham to enjoy the buffet featuring farm-raised catfish, broasted chicken, succulent ribs and, of course, barbecue. All-you-can-eat homemade ice cream from freezers powered by a one-cylinder, 1927 John Deere engine plus homemade cobblers make a great finish for a delicious meal at Barry's.

BUFFET HOURS:
Thursdays: 11:00 am to 1:00 pm and
5:00 pm to 7:00 pm
Fridays: 11:00 am to 1:00 pm and
4:30 pm to 7:30 pm
Saturdays: 4:00 pm to 7:30 pm

Jimbo's Bar-B-Q

161 11th Avenue West
Guin, AL 35563
205-468-2272

and Saturday nights. A local favorite is the Smothered Fries. You are sure to enjoy Jimbo's family-style atmosphere, so stop by and enjoy their outstanding homemade offerings.

Now Serving Breakfast
Monday – Thursday: 5:00 am to 2:00 pm
Friday & Saturday: 5:00 am to 8:00 pm
Sunday: 11:00 am to 2:00 pm

Serving the locals since 2008, Jimbo's makes all of their sauces from scratch including the barbecue sauce that has been perfected over many years by Jimbo himself. Jimbo's is also known for having the "Best Ribs Around," and their homemade banana pudding is one of the best in the South. Their country-style steam bar is open Wednesday, Thursday, Friday, and Sunday. Jimbo's famous grilled and fried fish plates are on order Friday

Rose's Strawberry Shortcake

Cake:

1 box classic white cake mix (plus ingredients to prepare per directions)

½ cup sour cream

Preheat oven 350°. Prepare cake batter per box directions adding ½ cup sour cream. Bake cake in Bundt pan using time guidelines on box, but remove cake 5 minutes before time on box. Cool.

Strawberry Icing:

1 cup sour cream

1 (16-ounce) box powdered sugar

1 (8-ounce) package cream cheese, softened

1 (8-ounce) carton Cool Whip

½ (12-ounce) package strawberry glaze

1 (8- to 10-ounce) package frozen strawberries

Combine sour cream, powdered sugar, cream cheese and Cool Whip; set aside. Combine glaze and strawberries; set aside.

Cut cooled cake horizontally and set top layer aside. Spread half the icing on bottom layer then top with half the strawberry mixture. Replace top layer and spread with remaining icing; top with remaining strawberry mixture, letting glaze run down the sides. Cut and ENJOY!

Restaurant Recipe

Crawmama's

Tequila Sanders Photography

5002 Webb Villa
Guntersville, AL 35976
256-582-0484
www.crawmamas.com

Crawmama's originally opened in 1987 as Crawdaddy's Seafood Shoppe. Charlotte Webb, founder and co-owner of the now-named Crawmama's, was born and raised right in Guntersville, Alabama. She grew up there knowing the area was in desperate need of a fresh seafood supplier. Now, many years later, Crawmama's seats 350 people and offers live entertainment on the weekends. The menu includes shrimp, oysters, crab legs, crawfish, fish, gator, and much more. With a tin roof, concrete floors, and picnic tables, you are sure to enjoy a unique dining experience.

Thursday & Friday: 4:30 pm to 10:00 pm
Saturday: 11:30 am to 10:00 pm

Jalapeño Hushpuppies

2 cups cornmeal

1 cup flour

2 eggs, beaten

3 teaspoons baking powder

1½ teaspoons salt

5 jalapeño peppers, chopped

1 small onion, minced

Buttermilk

Pinch baking soda

Heat oil in a deep fryer or pot to 350°. Mix all ingredients together using just enough buttermilk to make it the consistency of really thick cornbread batter. Using a small ice cream scoop to get a consistent shape and size, drop scoopfuls of batter into hot oil. Hushpuppies should float within 2 minutes or so after dropping in hot oil; turn hushpuppy to brown on other side. Remove to drain on paper towels to absorb excess oil.

Restaurant Recipe

Bacon-Wrapped Stuffed Jalapeño Peppers

18 large jalapeño peppers

2 (8-ounce) packages cream cheese, softened

4 large garlic cloves, minced

1 medium onion, minced

2 tablespoons finely chopped fresh cilantro

½ teaspoon coarse sea salt

1 pound bacon

Skewers, soak in water about 15 minutes

Heat grill to medium-high heat; place foil on grill to make cleanup a little easier. Slice jalapeños lengthwise; remove and discard seeds. (If you want these to be really spicy, don't remove the seeds.) Mix cream cheese, garlic, onion, cilantro and salt until well blended; set aside. Cook bacon until it is half-way done. (We cook ours the old-fashioned way but the microwave works just as well.) While bacon is cooling, begin stuffing your peppers by spooning mixture into each jalapeño half. Wrap a slice of bacon around each jalapeño and use a skewer to secure it in place. Grill your Bacon-Wrapped Stuffed Jalapeño Peppers until bacon is completely cooked (you may have to turn them several times). Serve immediately or at room temperature.

Restaurant Recipe

Homemade Key Lime Pie

5 egg yolks, beaten

1 (12-ounce) can sweetened condensed milk

¼ cup (2 ounces) heavy cream

½ cup key lime juice

1 (9-inch) graham cracker crust

Preheat oven to 375°. Combine egg yolks, sweetened condensed milk, heavy cream and lime juice; mix well. Pour into unbaked crust. Bake 15 minutes. Allow to cool. Top with whipped topping and lime slices before serving, if desired.

Restaurant Recipe

THINKSTOCK/ISTOCK/WILLIAM44

Rock House Eatery

1201 Gunter Avenue
Guntersville, AL 35976
256-505-4699
www.rockhouseeatery.com

Everything about the Rock House Eatery & Catering Company is easy on the senses—distinctive dishes created with the freshest ingredients, excellent service, a relaxing atmosphere, and prices that prove a great restaurant experience doesn't have to be hard on the card. Everything is homemade and fresh, with an emphasis on sustainable sources and a "local farm-to-table" philosophy. Whether it's a casual encounter with our famous Rockstar Roast Beef Sub, or getting serious with perfect steaks and seafood, the Rock House is solid. From simple starts to satisfying finishes, we invite you to visit the Rock House. It's an easy decision.

Tuesday – Sunday: 10:30 am to 2:00 pm
Wednesday – Saturday:
5:00 pm to 9:00 pm

Filet Mignon Beef Pot Pie

2 tablespoon olive oil

1½ pounds beef tenderloin, trimmed and cut into ½-inch pieces

4 tablespoons butter

1 cup chopped onion

4 teaspoons flour

4 cups low-sodium beef broth

2 cups diced carrots

2 cups diced potatoes

½ teaspoon thyme

1 (17.3-ounce) package frozen puff pastry or regular pastry crust

1 egg, beaten with 1 teaspoon water

Heat olive oil in large heavy pot over high heat until just smoking. Brown beef pieces; drain oil leaving beef in pot. Lower heat to medium-high; add butter and onions. When onions are translucent, stir in flour. Cook, stirring, 3 to 4 minutes. Stir in broth, continuing to stir until incorporated. Add vegetables and thyme. Simmer until vegetables are barely tender. Pour filling into a greased baking dish. Cover with a sheet of pastry, sealing edges onto sides of dish; poke holes into center for steam vents. Brush with beaten egg. Bake at 350° for 45 to 50 minutes, or until golden brown.

Restaurant Recipe

BUCK'S POCKET

Guntersville, Alabama

Buck's Pocket, a 2,000-acre park in northeast Alabama is secluded in a natural pocket of the Appalachian Mountains. Legend says that defeated politicians come here to "lick their wounds."

For more information go to: www.alapark.com

Table 6

429 Gunter Avenue • Guntersville, AL 35976
256-582-1676

Table 6 is about casual sophistication, outstanding service and amazing food. Preparing only the freshest, highest-quality food, Chef Jeremy South strives to ensure his guests all become Table 6 family. And it shows. From outstanding appetizers— Baked Fontina and Cajun Shrimp, to delicious main dishes—Center Cut Filet Mignon, Farm Fresh Chicken Breast and Lobster Tails with Drawn Butter, plus gourmet desserts, each meal at Table 6 is an experience not soon forgotten. Try Table 6 today and it will soon become your favorite restaurant, too.

Tuesday - Saturday: 5:00 pm to 10:00 pm

Razz-Tini

¾ ounce razzmatazz raspberry liquor

¼ ounce raspberry flavored vodka

1 ounce sour mixer

1 ounce cranberry juice

Splash Coca-Cola

Fresh or frozen raspberries, optional

Muddle all ingredients, except Coke and raspberries, in shaker with ice. Shake 32 times. Add a splash of Coca-Cola and pour into a frosted martini glass. Add raspberries and serve.

Restaurant Recipe

Lime Herb Vinaigrette

¼ cup Dijon mustard

2 cups olive oil

¼ cup lime juice

¼ cup German white wine

3 tablespoons honey

Splash hot sauce

2 tablespoons chopped parsley

2 tablespoons chopped chives

Salt and pepper to taste

Start with Dijon in a mixing bowl. Slowly add oil, whipping with a wire whisk until emulsified. Add lime juice, wine and honey blending with whisk. Add hot sauce, parsley, chives, salt and pepper; mix. Put in container and chill until ready to use.

Restaurant Recipe

Bama-Q Pit & Grill

125 Military Trail
Hamilton, AL 35570
205-921-0221

The Bama-Q is American owned and operated by the Montgomery Family. This restaurant was opened in 2008, but this family has been in the restaurant business for 25 years. Serving real pit barbecue, ribs, smoked chicken, brisket, great rib-eye steaks, catfish, and shrimp, their experience shows in every tasty bite. Come on by for the best home cooking.

Wednesday Lunch Buffet:
11:00 am to 2:00 pm
Thursday & Friday: 11:00 am to 9:00 pm
Saturday: 2:00 pm to 9:00 pm
Sunday: 11:00 am to 2:00 pm

Good Meatloaf

Meatloaf:

2 pounds ground beef

1 pound pork sausage

1 medium onion, diced

1 medium bell pepper, diced

½ cup oats or breadcrumbs

1 (10.75-ounce) can cream of mushroom soup

1 teaspoon Tony Chachere's Creole seasoning

2 eggs

3 tablespoons Worcestershire sauce

2 tablespoons yellow mustard

Topping:

½ cup ketchup

2 teaspoons horseradish

3 tablespoons brown sugar

Combine meatloaf ingredients; mix well. Put into loaf pan and bake at 350° for 1 hour. After meatloaf is cooked, combine topping ingredients. Spread over meatloaf and broil 2 to 5 minutes.

Restaurant Recipe

Chocolate Slab Cake

2 cups self-rising flour

2 cups sugar

4 tablespoons cocoa

1 cup water

2 sticks margarine

2 eggs, beaten

2 teaspoons vanilla extract

½ cup buttermilk

1 teaspoon baking soda

Combine flour, sugar and cocoa in a mixing bowl. Microwave water and margarine for 3 minutes. Add to flour mixture. Add remaining ingredients; beat 3 minutes with electric mixer. Pour into 9x13-inch baking pan and bake at 350° for 28 minutes.

Chocolate Icing:

1 stick margarine

4 tablespoons cocoa

6 tablespoons milk

1 (16-ounce) box powdered sugar

1 teaspoon vanilla extract

Add margarine, cocoa and milk to a saucepan. Cook over medium heat until it comes to a boil. Boil 2 minutes then remove from heat. Add powdered sugar and vanilla, beating well. Spread over cake while both cake and icing are hot. Leave in pan and cover with plastic wrap or foil. Serve warm with ice cream.

Restaurant Recipe

Plantation Potato Soup

4 cups diced potatoes

⅔ cup diced celery

1 medium onion, diced

1 gallon (16 cups) water

½ teaspoon salt

½ teaspoon pepper

1 stick butter

6 tablespoons flour

2 cups milk

Combine all ingredients, except flour and milk, and bring to a boil in a 2-gallon pot. Boil 10 minutes. Mix flour and milk; stir into soup. Simmer 10 minutes, stirring often. Let sit 10 minutes. Enjoy.

Restaurant Recipe

THINKSTOCK/ISTOCK/YELENAYEMCHUK

Tater Tot Casserole

Casserole:

1 (32-ounce) package tater tots

1 (16-ounce) carton sour cream

1 cup shredded cheese

1 (10.75-ounce) can cream of mushroom soup

2 teaspoons Tony Chachere's Creole seasoning

Topping:

1 sleeve Ritz crackers

1 stick butter, melted

Combine casserole ingredients; pour into casserole dish. Combine crackers and butter; spread over casserole. Bake 350° for 45 minutes.

**Bama-Q Pit & Grill
Restaurant Recipe**

Squash Casserole

6 medium squash, sliced

½ cup chopped onion

¼ cup chopped green pepper

½ cup mayonnaise

4 teaspoons sugar

2 eggs, beaten

1 teaspoon Tony Chachere's Creole seasoning

Mix everything together and place in casserole dish.

Topping:

¾ cup grated cheese

¾ stick margarine

¾ cup breadcrumbs

Mix topping together and sprinkle on top of casserole. Bake at 350° for 60 minutes.

**Bama-Q Pit & Grill
Restaurant Recipe**

THINKSTOCK/
ISTOCK/
ADLIFEMARKETING

Dinelli's Pizza & Pasta

1780 Military Street South
Hamilton , AL 35570
205-921-2106
www.dinellis.com

Dinelli's Pizza & Pasta is family owned and has been serving Hamilton and the surrounding areas since 1989. They serve up the best pizza around with hand-rolled dough, homemade sauce, and high-quality toppings. Enjoy slices from the all-you-can-eat lunch buffet which also includes pasta, garlic sticks, full salad bar, tacos, nachos, spaghetti, homemade peach cobbler, and drink. Or order a custom pizza from a full menu that includes pizzas, pastas, appetizers, salad bar, and much more. A local favorite is made-to-order sandwiches on bread baked from scratch daily using Dinelli's own recipe. Voted Best Restaurant in Marion County for 2013.

Monday, Tuesday, Thursday, Friday &
Saturday: 11:00 am to 8:30 pm
Sunday: 11:00 am to 2:30 pm

Chocolate Cobbler

2 sticks butter or margarine
1½ cups self-rising flour
2½ cups sugar, divided
¾ cup milk
½ teaspoon vanilla extract
6 tablespoons cocoa
2 cups cold water

Preheat oven to 350°. Melt butter in 9x13-inch pan. Combine flour, 1½ cups sugar, milk and vanilla. Pour into butter in pan. Combine remaining 1 cup sugar and cocoa; sprinkle over the top (do not stir). Pour cold water on top; do not stir. Bake 30 minutes; do not overcook.

Restaurant Recipe

Cabbage Bowl Restaurant

12070 Alabama Highway 75
Henagar, AL 35978
256-657-4191
www.cabbagebowlrestaurant.com

Cabbage Bowl Restaurant is owned and operated by Mike and Staci Pope. The restaurant opened nearly 20 years ago by Staci's two aunts and has become a family legacy. The Popes offer delicious southern country cooking in a cozy setting with friendly service. You'll be treated like family. As a matter of fact, Aunt Betty Jo lives right down the road, comes in almost daily for a cup of coffee and is glad to pitch in anytime she's needed. So, drop by for some home cooking.

Monday: 6:00 am to 2:00 pm
Tuesday – Sunday: 6:00 am to 8:00 pm

Stuffed Pepper Cups

6 medium green bell peppers
1 pound ground beef
½ cup chopped onion
2 (14-ounce) cans stewed tomatoes
¾ cup rice
2 tablespoons Worcestershire sauce
Salt and pepper
1 cup shredded sharp American cheese, plus more for top

Cut tops from bell peppers; remove seeds and membranes. Precook peppers in boiling salted water about 5 minutes; drain. Sprinkle inside with salt and set aside.

Brown meat and onion; drain. Add tomatoes, rice and Worcestershire; mix well. Season to taste with salt and pepper and bring heat up to high. Reduce heat to simmer, cover and cook until rice is almost tender, about 5 minutes. Add cheese.

Stuff peppers. Stand upright in 10x6-inch baking dish. Bake uncovered in 350° oven for 25 minutes or until hot. Sprinkle with more cheese. Serves 6

Restaurant Recipe

Texas Brownies

2 cups flour

2 cups sugar

½ cup butter

½ cup shortening

1 cup strong brewed coffee or water

¼ cup dark unsweetened cocoa

½ cup buttermilk

2 eggs

1 teaspoon baking soda

1 teaspoon vanilla extract

Frosting:

½ cup butter

2 tablespoons dark cocoa

¼ cup milk

3½ cups powdered sugar

1 teaspoon vanilla extract

In large mixing bowl, combine flour and sugar. In heavy saucepan, combine butter, shortening, coffee and cocoa; bring to a boil. Pour over flour and sugar; stir. Add buttermilk, eggs, baking soda and vanilla. Mix well, using a wooden spoon or electric mixer. Pour into a well-buttered 11x17½-inch jelly roll pan. Bake at 400° for 20 minutes or until brownies test done in the center.

While brownies bake, prepare frosting. In saucepan, combine butter, cocoa and milk. Heat to boiling, stirring constantly. Remove from heat and immediately add powdered sugar and vanilla; mix vigorously until frosting is smooth.

Pour warm frosting over brownies as soon as you take them out of the oven.

Restaurant Recipe

Mud Creek Fishing Camp Restaurant

844 County Road 213
Hollywood, AL 35752
256-259-2493

This casual-dining, family-owned restaurant is located about 100 yards from the water of the Mud Creek Slough. Everything is priced right and delicious, so you may want to try their hand-breaded chicken fingers and shrimp, grilled fish, steaks or their variety of sandwiches and salads. We highly recommend Mud Creek's specialties—the barbecue pork and fried catfish. Their barbecue is cooked just like it was in 1947 when the restaurant first opened for business—on a pit with live hickory coals. Delicious!

Tuesday – Saturday: 11:00 am to 8:00 pm
Sunday: 11:00 am to 3:00 pm

Mud Creek Baked Beans

1 (7-pound) can pork and beans

1 cup chopped bell pepper

1 cup chopped onion

½ pound barbecued pork or beef, shredded small

2 cups sweet barbecue sauce

½ cup (¼ pound) brown sugar

Mix all ingredients; bake at 325° for 45 minutes. Makes about 25 servings.

Restaurant Recipe

Buttermilk Fruit Salad

2 (5.1-ounce) boxes vanilla instant pudding

6 cups buttermilk

1 (12-ounce) carton whipped topping

2 (15- to 16-ounce) cans fruit cocktail, drained

Mix pudding according to directions using buttermilk in place of whole milk. Stir in whipped topping. Add drained fruit cocktail; stir just until mixed.

Restaurant Recipe

Talk of the Town Baked Beans

2 gallons baked beans

1 cup yellow mustard

1 cup pancake syrup

2 cups barbeque sauce

2 cups diced onion

2 cups diced green bell pepper

1 pound smoked pulled pork

Combine all ingredients in a large pot over medium-low heat. Keep hot until ready to serve.

Restaurant Recipe

Chef Troy's Talk of the Town Restaurant

**4815 County Road 63
Houston, AL 35572
205-489-1700 • 205-489-9318
www.cheftroystalkofthetown.com**

Chef Troy's Talk of the Town is very deceiving at first glance because it is located in a building that used to be a country gas station. Once inside, however, you get a lot more than expected. Chef Troy is frequently walking around greeting customers, filling drinks, pulling plates, and making conversation. If it is your first time to dine there, and Chef Troy knows this, he will fill you up on samples. So if you are ever in Houston, Alabama, be sure to drop in and try some of Chef Troy's original recipes.

**Sunday – Wednesday: 6:30 am to 2:00 pm
Thursday – Saturday: 6:30 am to 9:00 pm**

Cotton Row Restaurant

100 South Side Square • Huntsville, AL 35801
256-382-9500
www.cottonrowrestaurant.com

Nestled on the southwest corner of the Courthouse Square, the three-story brick building that houses Cotton Row Restaurant was built in 1821 along the cotton exchange. Cotton Row was Chef James Boyce's first of six restaurants to open in Huntsville in 2008. This flagship restaurant offers an ever-changing menu of inventive dishes that showcase the finest local and seasonal ingredients. A vision for comfort, elegance, and modern American cuisine, inspired by the enduring passion of cotton traders who once worked in downtown Huntsville, is the passion of Cotton Row. Experience their southern hospitality.

Lunch, Wednesday – Friday: 11:00 am to 2:00 pm
Dinner, Monday – Saturday: 5:00 pm to 10:00 pm
Sunday Brunch: 10:30 am to 3:00 pm

Braised Beef Short Ribs in Red Wine and Pomegranate

3 pounds beef short ribs (cleaned)

Salt and freshly ground pepper

½ cup all-purpose flour

3 tablespoons olive oil

1 tablespoon sweet butter

1 small onion, diced

2 stalks celery, diced

4 garlic cloves, crushed

½ (26-ounce) bottle dry red wine (3¼ cups)

1 cup pomegranate juice

1 quart (4 cups) veal stock (beef broth)

1 bouquet garni (bay leaf, thyme, rosemary, parsley)

¼ cup pomegranate seeds

Place short ribs on baking sheet pan and dry well with paper towels. Season both sides with salt and freshly ground pepper. Dust ribs completely with flour and brush off extra.

Heat thick-bottom cast-iron pot over medium heat with olive oil. Place ribs into pot and brown evenly, about 3 to 4 minutes on each side. Add butter, onion, celery and garlic; cook an additional 2 minutes, browning vegetables lightly.

Remove excess grease from pot and slowly add wine and pomegranate juice. Continue to cook slowly until liquid is reduced by half. Add veal stock and bouquet garni and bring mixture to simmer. Cover pot and continue to simmer (cooking slowly) over low heat; or place pot into a pre-heated 300° oven and cook until ribs are tender, approximately 2 hours.

Remove from oven and cool to room temperature. Once cool, carefully remove meat from pot and strain liquid through a fine strainer into another pot. Return liquid to heat and cook until gravy consistency is reached. Return meat back to liquid, warm thoroughly, and serve with favorite starch and vegetables. Sprinkle with pomegranate seeds to finish.

Serves 6.

Chef James Boyce
Restaurant Recipe

Greenbrier Restaurant

27028 Old Highway 20
Madison, AL 35756
256-351-1800
www.oldgreenbrier.com

Greenbrier Restaurant specializes in catfish, seafood, and barbecue. Owned by the Evans family, Greenbrier is in a building originally built in 1952. Even though the kitchen was completely updated, the original rustic décor is intact in the dining rooms. In the early years country music stars sat on top of the building to sing to the crowds. Back in the good ole days they kept river fish in a barrel out back until they were ordered by the customers; today only pond-raised, grain-fed catfish are served. Thank goodness some things have changed. Don't miss stopping at Greenbrier—it's an experience.

Open 7 days a week:
10:00 am to 8:30 pm

White Sauce

1 pint (2 cups) white vinegar

1 pint (2 cups) salad dressing (not mayonnaise)

2 ounces (4 tablespoons) ground black pepper

Combine all ingredients. Some people like it thinner or thicker; you can adjust your portions of vinegar or salad dressing to your taste.

This is the easiest recipe for white sauce. Most people put it on barbecued chicken and barbecued ham, but you can put in on anything—baked potatoes, French fries, hushpuppies, and more. Enjoy!

Restaurant Recipe

SALLIE HOWARD MEMORIAL CHAPEL
Mentone, Alabama

Sallie Howard Memorial Chapel in Mentone was built in 1937 by Colonel Milford Howard as a memorial to his first wife. The stone church is built around a huge boulder that serves as the pulpit. The inscription "God has all ways been as good to me as I would let Him be" hangs over the pulpit and came from a letter to Howard from his wife.

Wildflower Café & Country Store

6007 AL Highway 117 • Mentone, AL 35984
256-634-0066 • www.mentonewildflower.com

Wildflower Café & Country Store won best destination restaurant in Rome, Georgia for 2012 and Best Atmosphere for 2012/2013 Dekalb, AL. It is shabby-chic and casual and simply serves the most wonderful food, combining the best cuisine from America, Greece, France, Italy, Asian, and Latin cultures into gourmet fusion dishes. Local favorites include their signature Tomato Pie, Brunch Sampler, fresh ground steak burgers, tender grilled steaks and fresh wild caught salmon. When in Mentone, don't miss Wildflower for the full experience of local food, music, and art in an award-winning atmosphere.

SEASONAL HOURS
For more information, visit
www.mentonewildflower.com

Wildflower Crêpes

Delicious French pastries with a southern twist

Crêpes:

16 eggs

8 cups flour

4 cups cool water

4 cups heavy cream

½ pound butter

Pinch salt

Combine all ingredients. Heat a 9-inch skillet or crêpe pan over medium heat. Treat with nonstick pan spray. Pour ¼ cup mixture into pan and spread by rolling skillet to spread batter thinly over hot skillet.

Cook on first side until stiff or easy to flip. Gently lift edge with thin spatula and flip. Cook 30 more seconds and place on wax paper. Crêpes can be stacked on top of each other with wax paper between each. Fill with Sweet Filling topped with Sweet Topping or use the Savory Filling.

Sweet Filling:

4 pounds cream cheese, softened

2 cups powdered sugar

1 tablespoon vanilla extract

Combine Sweet Filling ingredients. Spread about 4 tablespoons on left side of crêpe and roll to the right.

Sweet Topping:

Frozen sweetened and sliced strawberries, thawed

Chocolate sauce

Drain strawberries well; purée in blender. Serve over crêpes drizzled with chocolate sauce for a decadent delicious dessert crêpe.

Savory Filling:

1 pound seasoned baked salmon

2 tablespoons minced garlic

1 teaspoon cayenne pepper

8 (8-ounce) packages cream cheese, softened

1 tablespoon garlic powder

¼ cup caper berries

2 cups finely diced fresh spinach

1 cup finely diced sun-dried tomato

Combine savory filling ingredients. Spread about 6 tablespoons on left side of crêpe and roll to the right. Top with your favorite pesto recipe or cream sauce.

Restaurant Recipe

John's BBQ

15165 Court Street
Moulton, AL 35650
256-974-7721

12403 AL Highway 157
Moulton, AL 35650
256-974-8880
www.johns-log-cabin-bbq.com

For delicious barbecue served in the old tradition, visit John's BBQ. They do it right by continuing the tradition first started by the Woodall's barbecue. From vinegar slaw to slabs of ribs all served by a friendly staff, John's is the best in the land. Their world-famous Alabama white sauce served over chicken is a culinary treat, and another local favorite is their red sauce for pork. There are two locations, seating 50 diners and offering drive thru service. Their original location, "The Old Log Cabin," was built in the early 1800's. You can still see the hand-hewed logs.

Monday – Saturday:
10:00 am to 8:00 pm

North Alabama White Sauce

2 cups mayonnaise

1 cup white vinegar

¼ cup black pepper

¼ cup lemon juice

1 cup sugar

Mix and serve over grilled chicken. Also can be used as a dip.

Restaurant Recipe

Swamp John's Restaurants and Catering, Inc.

TWO LOCATIONS:
210 Woodward Ave. • Muscle Shoals
256-381-2722

5181 Highway 24 • Red Bay
256-356-2300

www.swampjohnscatfish.com

At Swamp John's, there's always more fish to fry. That's because they specialize in deep-fried catfish—the best catfish around. In addition to catfish, Swamp John's serves up crawfish, shrimp, chicken, po' boys, gumbo, jambalaya, and burgers along with delicious sides and homemade desserts. Locals and visitors alike can never pass up stopping at Swamp John's for a generous serving of catfish and hushpuppies. What's the secret recipe to Swamp John's delicious catfish? "We can't say what it is," owner John Shewbart says. "We just serve good quality food at a fair price."

Hours vary by location, call or go online for more details.

Fresh Apple Cake

2 cups sugar

1 cup vegetable oil

2 whole eggs

½ cup buttermilk

3 cups plain flour

1 teaspoon salt

1½ teaspoons baking soda

1 teaspoon cinnamon

2 teaspoons vanilla extract

3 cups chopped fresh apples

1 cup chopped nuts

1 cup coconut

Cream together sugar, oil, eggs and buttermilk. Add mixture of flour, salt, soda and cinnamon; mix well. Add vanilla, apples, nuts and coconut; mix well. Pour into a tube pan that has been greased and lined with wax paper. Bake at 350° for 1½ hours.

Freda Masterson
Grandmother of Matt Cooper,
partner in Swamp John's Restaurant

Brooks Barbeque

"SERVING THE SHOALS SINCE 1965"

203 Union Avenue
Muscle Shoals, AL 35661
256-381-1491
www.brooksbarbeque.weebly.com

Owned and operated by Ann Brooks Banksden and Lanndrea Banksden, Brooks Barbeque is well-known for original hickory smoked barbeque, chicken, ribs, wings, turkey, ham, and their famous hot dogs. Their homemade hot sauce and white sauce will top off your meal deliciously. For the side, you can't beat Brooks' homemade baked beans and potato salad. Their homemade slaw—regular, hot, and mild— are so unique and delicious they are sold in local Foodland Stores. Definitely save room for dessert—fresh baked sweet potato, coconut, and pecan pies.

Monday – Saturday: 10:00 am to 8:00 pm
Sunday: 11:00 am to 6:00 pm

Banana Pudding

⅓ cup all-purpose flour

⅔ cup plus ¼ cup sugar, divided

2 cups whole milk

2 eggs, separated

½ teaspoon vanilla extract

1 (12-ounce) box vanilla wafers

4 whole bananas, sliced

½ teaspoon cream of tartar

In heavy saucepan, combine flour and ⅔ cup sugar. Mix well. Gradually stir in milk and egg yolks. Stir constantly over medium heat until pudding thickens. Cool mixture slightly then stir in vanilla. Arrange a layer of vanilla wafers in bottom of 8-inch-square baking dish. Add a layer of bananas using about half, then cover with about half of pudding. Repeat layers. Beat egg whites until soft peaks form. Add cream of tartar and remaining ¼ cup sugar, 1 tablespoon at a time, beating until stiff peaks form. Spread over pudding sealing the edges. Bake at 350° approximately 10 to 12 minutes or until top turns golden brown. Makes 4 to 6 servings.

Restaurant Recipe

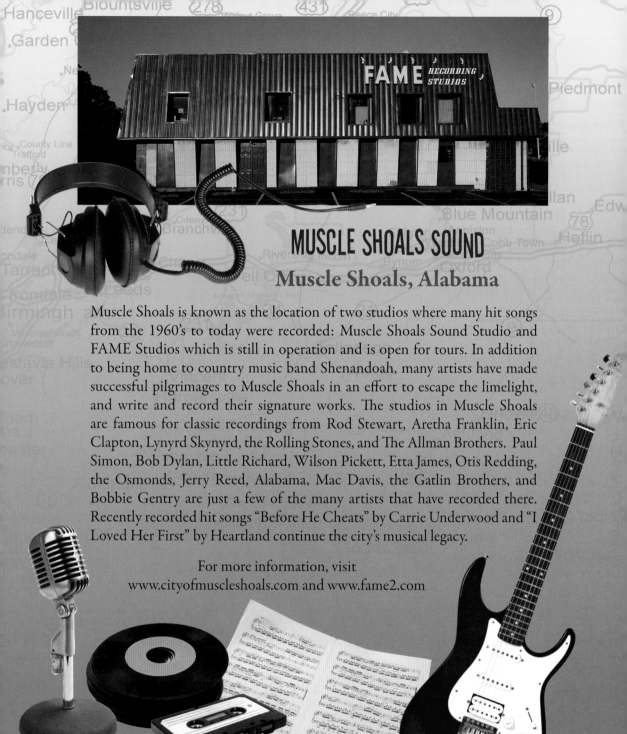

MUSCLE SHOALS SOUND
Muscle Shoals, Alabama

Muscle Shoals is known as the location of two studios where many hit songs from the 1960's to today were recorded: Muscle Shoals Sound Studio and FAME Studios which is still in operation and is open for tours. In addition to being home to country music band Shenandoah, many artists have made successful pilgrimages to Muscle Shoals in an effort to escape the limelight, and write and record their signature works. The studios in Muscle Shoals are famous for classic recordings from Rod Stewart, Aretha Franklin, Eric Clapton, Lynyrd Skynyrd, the Rolling Stones, and The Allman Brothers. Paul Simon, Bob Dylan, Little Richard, Wilson Pickett, Etta James, Otis Redding, the Osmonds, Jerry Reed, Alabama, Mac Davis, the Gatlin Brothers, and Bobbie Gentry are just a few of the many artists that have recorded there. Recently recorded hit songs "Before He Cheats" by Carrie Underwood and "I Loved Her First" by Heartland continue the city's musical legacy.

For more information, visit
www.cityofmuscleshoals.com and www.fame2.com

NEW MARKET BBQ

5601 Winchester Road
New Market, AL 35761
256-379-5525
www.newmarketbbq.com

Established in 1995 and located in the historic small town of New Market, New Market BBQ offers the best Old-School Hickory Pit Smoked Barbeque found in the Huntsville area. Step back in time and enjoy an old-fashioned meal on the screened-in porch or a picnic under the pavilion. Experience fresh-off-the-pit Hickory Smoked BBQ, as well as made-from-scratch sides and desserts. Our Smoked Mac n' Cheese is a MUST try!! Proud *Taste of Huntsville* Winners!

Experience the Difference and become a FAN. Checkout www.newmarketbbqfanpage.com for hours and customer reviews.

Old–Fashioned Peanut Butter Pie

1 cup powdered sugar
½ cup peanut butter
1 (9-inch) deep-dish pie shell, baked
½ cup all-purpose flour
¾ cup plus ¼ cup sugar (for meringue)
Pinch salt
2¼ cups milk, divided
1½ tablespoons margarine, melted
¾ tablespoon vanilla extract
3 eggs, separated

In a small bowl, knead powdered sugar and peanut butter (wearing disposable gloves) until mixture is crumbly. Place ½ mixture in bottom of baked pie shell; reserve the rest. In large saucepan, whisk together flour, sugar, and salt; stir in ½ cup milk to form a paste. Whisk in melted margarine and vanilla until well combined. Whisk in lightly beaten egg yolks, and then whisk in remaining milk. Cook over medium heat until thick, stirring constantly. Pour over peanut butter crumbles in pie crust. Make a meringue by beating egg whites until foamy. Add ¼ cup sugar; continue beating until soft peaks form. Spread over pie, sealing the edges. Sprinkle remaining peanut butter crumbles over top. Bake at 325° for 20 to 30 minutes. Refrigerate several hours before serving. ENJOY!

Restaurant Recipe

BBQ Sketti
(Barbeque Spaghetti)

1 large (45-ounce) jar Prego spaghetti sauce

1 to 2 (21-ounce) bottles Hunts Hickory Barbecue Sauce, divided

1 medium to large onion, chopped

1 medium to large bell pepper, chopped

1 cup grated Parmesan cheese

2 teaspoons garlic salt

2 (16-ounce) sleeves spaghetti noodles

1 pound pulled pork, chicken or beef brisket barbecue, chopped

2 cups shredded mozzarella cheese

In a large stock pot, combine spaghetti sauce and 1 bottle barbecue sauce. (Add a little water to each jar, shake and empty into pot so not to waste anything.) Stir well. Add onion, bell pepper, Parmesan cheese, garlic salt and any additional seasoning you prefer. Cook over medium heat, stirring occasionally, until onions and peppers are soft. Give the sauce a taste and if it is not as strong as you'd like, feel free to add more barbecue sauce. If you like a little heat, add some cayenne or hot sauce.

While sauce cooks, boil spaghetti noodles per package directions. When onions and peppers are soft, add chopped meat; blend well. Cook over low to medium heat, stirring frequently, another 10 to 15 minutes. Drain noodles completely. Fold into sauce. Remove from heat and stir in mozzarella You can pour into baking dish and bake with some more cheese on top if you wish, but it's ready to eat now! ENJOY!

Make this recipe your own by trying different sauces, seasonings, or meats to create unique dishes every time. In the restaurant, we pit smoke our BBQ Sketti for 30 minutes before serving just to add that extra layer of smoke flavor.

Restaurant Recipe

Best of Both Worlds Coleslaw

In the South you usually have to choose between vinegar slaw or mayonnaise slaw. Our recipe has some of both tastes in it as well as a refreshing and sweet finish!

Slaw Mix:

½ cup sugar

¼ cup white vinegar

4 cups mayonnaise

4 cups milk

Mix together with a whisk, let stand a few minutes and whisk again to make sure it is completely blended.

Coleslaw:

3 heads cabbage, finely shredded (keep a few of the darker green leaves for good color)

¼ cup dill pickle relish

Combine cabbage, relish and Slaw Mix. Refrigerate until ready to serve.

Restaurant Recipe

Ole Hickory BBQ

**5061 Maysville Road
New Market, AL 35761
(256) 859-2824
www.olehickorybbq.com**

You know that feeling you get when you walk into a place that feels familiar? Where your name is known and the foods you love are available? Well, Ole Hickory BBQ is that kind of place. The meats are slowly smoked for hours, each and every potato is hand-peeled for potato salad, and the homemade desserts . . . scrumptious. Whether you dine outside under the big old oak tree, on the screened-in porch, or in the dining room, you will definitely enjoy Ole Hickory's country charm.

**Wednesday – Saturday:
11:00 am to 7:00 pm
Sunday: 11:00 am to 2:00 pm**

Kielbasa with Peppers and Onions

1 pound kielbasa, 1-inch slices

1 large onion, ½-inch slices

1 large red bell pepper, ½-inch slices

1 large green bell pepper, ½-inch slices

1½ cups Steak Marinade (recipe follows)

Combine all ingredients in a large pot. Cook over medium-high heat, covered, for 20 minutes, stirring occasionally. Do not over cook; vegetables should still have a little crunch.

Steak Marinade:

¼ cup vegetable oil

½ cup Kikkoman soy sauce

½ cup LaChoy soy sauce

¼ cup Worcestershire sauce

½ cup fresh lemon juice

½ cup vinegar

¼ cup red wine

¾ tablespoon dry mustard

1 clove garlic, minced

1 teaspoon coarse ground black pepper

Mix well and store in sealed jar in refrigerator for up to a month. Makes 3 cups.

Restaurant Recipe

Charlie B's

**300 6th Street South
Oneonta, AL 35121
205-274-7427
www.charliebsrestaurant.com**

Charlie B's is a lunchtime institution in Oneonta. The restaurant draws customers from all over North Alabama. It is the type of buffet restaurant that salesmen reschedule their route around to make sure they can dine there on certain menu days. Serving the best in traditional southern cuisine and a little of the new, Charlie B's definitely lives up to their motto: "Southern Dining at Its Finest."

**Lunch: 7 days a week
11:00 am to 2:00 pm
Dinner: Friday only
5:00 pm to 9:00 pm
Breakfast: Saturday only
7:00 am to 10:00 am**

256-356-2226

Fourth Street Grill & Steakhouse

607 4th Street
Red Bay, AL 35582
www.facebook.com/fourthstreetgrill

Fourth Street Grill & Steakhouse is owned and operated by Brent and Lorie Collum. They pride themselves on serving the freshest produce and meats available, buying locally-grown produce from Alabama, Mississippi, Tennessee, and Georgia. You will definitely enjoy their ribeyes, New York strips, and sirloins— available in different sizes and cut from the loin daily. Local favorites include their 30+-item salad bar and homemade pecan pies (when available). As they say, "You won't find any imitation products here!"

Tuesday – Thursday: 10:30 am to 9:00 pm
Friday & Saturday: 10:30 am to 10:00 pm
Sunday: 10:30 am to 9:00 pm

Jalapeño Corn

2 (15-ounce) cans whole-kernel corn, drained

1 (8-ounce) package cream cheese, softened

5 jalapeño slices
(from a jar of sliced jalapeños)

1 tablespoon jalapeño juice
(from a jar of sliced jalapeños)

Heat corn and cream cheese over medium heat until hot through and through. Stir in jalapeños and juice. Serve immediately. The longer it sits the hotter it gets.

Family Favorite

Pecan Pie

4 eggs

1 stick butter, melted

1 cup Karo syrup

1 tablespoon vinegar

1 cup brown sugar

Dash salt

1½ cups pecans

1 (9-inch) pie crust

Mix all ingredients, except pie crust, together. Pour in pie crust. Bake at 350° for 1 hour.

Restaurant Recipe

McCutchen's Magnolia House

**303 East Willow Street
Scottsboro, AL 35768
256-259-3077**

Located just off the historic square of Scottsboro, Magnolia House was opened by Bill and Gene McCutchen in June of 2010, in the late 19th century home built by their maternal grandfather, J.D. Snodgrass who was mayor of the town for 42 years. The historic house is decorated to create the feel of that golden era in American history and affords customers the comfort and style of a gracious southern home. The restaurant offers a buffet of "down-home" favorites which change daily or diners may select from a menu with various appetizers, salads, and sandwiches. Desserts baked in-house are a variety of cakes, pies, and cobblers.

7 days a week: 11:00 am to 2:00 pm

Vinegar Pie

1 stick butter, melted and cooled

2 tablespoons flour

1½ cups sugar

1 tablespoon vanilla extract

2 tablespoons vinegar

3 eggs

1 (9-inch) pie crust, baked

Combine butter, flour, sugar, vanilla, vinegar and eggs; mix well. Pour into pie shell. Bake at 350° for 45 minutes. Cool before cutting. Yields 6 slices.

Restaurant Recipe

Sweet Tater Dumplings

1 (8-count) package round yam patties

1 (8-ounce) can crescent rolls

1 cup water

1 cup sugar combined with
2 tablespoons cinnamon
(or your preferred ratio)

1 stick margarine

1 tablespoon cornstarch

1 teaspoon vanilla extract

Preheat oven to 350°. Wrap each yam with a crescent roll and place in a cake pan. In a saucepan, combine remaining ingredients and bring to a boil. Pour over yams and bake 45 minutes.

Family Recipe

50 Taters

24961 John T. Reid Parkway
Scottsboro, AL 35768
256-259-3222
Wednesday: 11:00 am to 3:00 pm
Thursday – Saturday: 11:00 am to 8:00 pm
Sunday: 11:00 am to 2:30 pm

770 East Main Street
Rainsville, AL 35986
256-638-3150
Monday – Saturday: 10:00 am to 8:00 pm
Sunday: 10:00 am to 2:30 pm

At 50 Taters, you are guaranteed "Good Eats in the 'Boro." Their over-sized sandwiches are the best anywhere, but their "loaded baked taters" are the star of the show. Try one with anything from pork barbeque to lobster, all served with 50 Taters homemade sauces. Try a delicious sandwich of the day or one of sixteen other favorite sandwiches. In a hurry? The plate lunch is super-fast but tastes great. Don't miss Prime Rib on Friday and come back Saturday for Steak & Ribs Day. It's all good at 50 Taters.

Chief & Snoogie's Hickory Pit BBQ

23419 Alabama Highway 24 • Trinity, AL 35673
256-351-9904 • www.chiefandsnoogiebbq.com

If you are looking for authentic Alabama barbecue, be sure to stop by Chief & Snoogie's. These two friends are serving up outstanding barbecue and delicious sides 7 days a week. The meat is smoked on-site daily so it is fresh and tastes great. Their wood building is decorated inside with a selection of nice memorabilia. That antique glass-topped gas pump is not to be missed when you visit. But it's

the food that will keep you coming back. Their pulled pork is exquisite, but you are sure to enjoy everything you try. Expect a lot of food for a great price and a friendly attentive staff, too. Chief & Snoogie know great barbecue.

Monday – Saturday: 11:00 am to 8:00 pm
Sundays: 11:00 am to 3:00 pm

Black Bottom Pie

Crust:

1¼ cups gingersnap cookie crumbs

1½ sticks butter, softened

Preheat oven to 350°. Combine cookie crumbs and butter; press into bottom and sides of 9-inch pie plate. Bake 12 minutes.

Filling:

2 cups milk

1 envelope unflavored gelatin

4 eggs, separated

⅔ cup sugar

1 heaping tablespoon cornstarch

2 squares unsweetened baking chocolate, shaved

¼ cup rum

Scald milk then set aside to cool slightly. Dissolve gelatin in 1 cup water; set aside. Beat eggs yolks then add a little scalded milk to temper them. Add egg yolk mixture to remaining scalded milk along with sugar and cornstarch. Beat to make a custard until mixture coats spoon. Place shaved chocolate in a 2-cup measuring cup. Pour hot custard over chocolate to ¾ cup; stir. Spread chocolate custard over crust; refrigerate.

Add dissolved gelatin to remaining custard and cool to room temperature (about 30 minutes). Once cooled, stir in ¼ cup rum. Beat egg whites and fold into custard. Spread over chocolate layer and chill at least 30 minutes.

Topping:

1 cup heavy cream

1 heaping tablespoon sugar

Whip cream and sugar until thick; spread over pie. Grate additional chocolate over top, if desired. Chill 1 hour or until ready to serve.

Local Favorite

Rocking Chair Restaurant

814 US 72
Tuscumbia, AL 35674
256-381-6105

If you are looking for good country-style cooking, Rocking Chair Restaurant is the place for you. No matter the day of the week or the time of the day, you will always find great country food in generous portions, good service, down-home ambiance, and friendly service. Their catfish is a local favorite, but there is a lot to choose from and all delicious. So, come on in, have a seat, and get fed.

Sunday – Thursday: 7:00 am to 8:00 pm
Friday & Saturday: 7:00 am to 9:00 pm

Rocking Chair Pineapple Casserole

3 (15-ounce) cans pineapple chunks, with juice

1 cup sugar

1 cup melted butter

½ cup self-rising flour

2 cups shredded Cheddar cheese

Topping:

2 cups breadcrumbs

½ cup melted butter

Drain juice from pineapples, reserving juice. Combine pineapple juice, sugar, melted butter and flour; beat with wire whip until smooth and there are no lumps. Add cheese and pineapple; mix well. Spray bottom and sides of large baking dish with nonstick spray. Pour mixture in and smooth out. Combine topping ingredients and spread over pineapple mixture. Bake at 350° for 30 minutes.

Restaurant Recipe

THINKSTOCK/ISTOCK

Sweet Potato Casserole

Casserole:

3 medium sweet potatoes, baked

2 eggs, beaten

¾ cup sugar

½ cup margarine

1 teaspoon vanilla extract

Mash sweet potatoes to make 3 cups. Stir in remaining casserole ingredients until well mixed. Pour in a buttered 11x13-inch casserole dish.

Topping:

1 cup light brown sugar

⅓ cup plain flour

1 cup chopped nuts

2 to 4 tablespoons margarine

Combine brown sugar, flour and nuts. Spread over casserole. Dot with margarine and bake at 350° for 30 minutes.

Restaurant Recipe

Burgers & More

488 Bankhead Highway
Winfield, AL 35594
205-487-4408

Burgers & More is a café-style restaurant that has been in operation more than 20 years. Open seven days a week and offering a variety of delicious foods, they are best known for their chicken tenders and burgers. Located in midtown Winfield, Burgers & More offers a friendly and cozy environment plus reasonable prices and a kids menu. Their specialty trays are great for all occasions and they do prepared foods for any event. Stop by when you are in the area and check them out.

Monday – Saturday: 9:00 am to 9:00 pm

Metropolitan REGION

THINKSTOCK/ISTOCK

Joe's Italian Pizza, Pasta & Caffe

21 Weatherly Club Drive
Alabaster, AL 35007
205-663-4111
www.joesitalianonline.com

The original Joe's Italian Pizza, Pasta & Caffe opened in 1981 in Gilroy, California by Guiseppe and Elvira Bertolone. After moving to Alabama for retirement, they opened the new restaurant with their family. Collectively, they share with you their love and passion for Italian culture and cuisine. They believe in fresh food, prepared with only the best ingredients, and only serve real Italian culture and cuisine to their guests. They also believe in excellent customer service in a clean and friendly family atmosphere. The real pleasure comes when you first taste Mamma's authentic Old World cooking. Only the freshest ingredients accompany Mamma's century-old recipes to give patrons a little bit of Italy in Alabaster.

Monday – Sunday: 10:30 am to 9:00 pm

Joe's Italian Tomato Basil Soup

2 tablespoons butter
2 tablespoons olive oil
1 large yellow onion, chopped
1 tablespoon minced fresh garlic
4 cups ground tomatoes
1 cup chicken broth
1 teaspoon oregano
Salt and pepper to taste
¼ cup chopped fresh basil
½ cup heavy cream or half-and-half

Melt the butter with the oil over low heat in a heavy-bottom pot. Add the onion; wilt over low heat for 8 to 10 minutes. Add the garlic during the last 2 minutes, stirring. Add the tomatoes and broth. Bring to a boil, reduce heat to a simmer and cover; cook over medium-low heat for 60 minutes. Season with oregano, salt and pepper. Add basil. Stir in the cream or half-and-half, simmer for another 30 minutes. Garnish with fresh basil before serving.

Note: When tomatoes are in season use fresh tomatoes, blanch for 8 minutes and process with food processor. In the winter, use a San Marzano-type canned tomato, drain half of the liquid and process in food processor.

Restaurant Recipe

Linda's Squash Casserole

1 large onion, chopped

1 stick butter

8 ounces water

8 cups (about 2 cooked pans) cornbread, crumbled

1½ (10.75-ounce) cans cream of chicken soup

4 cups sliced cooked squash

½ teaspoon black pepper

⅛ teaspoon sage

8 ounces grated cheese

Cook onion in butter and water. In a large bowl, combine cornbread, soup, squash, pepper and sage. Add cheese and onion mixture. Put in large baking dish and bake at 350° for 50 minutes.

Restaurant Recipe

Sho'Nuff BBQ

651 Alexander City Shopping Center Drive
Alexander City, AL 35010
256-234-7675

Started in 1990 by Gerald Atchison, Sho'Nuff is well known for its Sho'Nuff Tater as well as southern vegetables. We are here to please the whole family with a variety of foods to satisfy all tastes. While you are here, be sure to try Linda's homemade desserts. Located in the Alexander Shopping Center, we are a family-friendly restaurant and one of the top ten restaurants featured in the documentary "A Taste of Hog Heaven" by Max Shores. Come by and visit. We will treat you like family. We cater. Give us a call.

Monday – Saturday: 10:00 am to 8:00 pm
Closed Sundays

Chocolate Fudge Pie

¼ cup cocoa

¼ cup flour

1¼ cups sugar

4 eggs, beaten

¼ cup butter, melted

1 teaspoon vanilla extract

1 (8-inch) pie shell

Mix first 3 ingredients together. Add eggs and butter; Mix well. Stir in vanilla. Pour in pie shell and bake 20 minutes at 350°. Cut and serve hot with ice cream and chocolate syrup.

Restaurant Recipe

Gates Restaurant

404 3rd Avenue Northwest
Aliceville, AL 35442
205-373-8100

Gates Restaurant is family owned and operated since 1958, originally by Owen and Ruth Gates in the 1980's, then Ken and Tim Gates took over and cooked for about 20 years. They closed for a short time to have their families and now Tim and wife Angie have relocated and reopened in the same town as the original Gates Restaurant was started. They still slow roast the prime rib and hand cut rib-eye steaks on Friday and Saturday nights as well as hand-batter all the fried foods as they are ordered.

LUNCH: Tuesday – Saturday
11:00 am to 2:00 pm
DINNER: Friday & Saturday
5:00 pm to 9:00 pm

High Points' Tuna Salad

2 (5-ounce) cans water-packed light tuna, well drained

1 (5-ounce) can water-packed albacore tuna, well drained

Lemon pepper to taste (unsalted is best)

¼ cup chopped apple (do not peel)

2 tablespoons mayonnaise

2 tablespoons sweet pickle relish

2 to 3 tablespoons chopped celery

2 to 3 tablespoons sliced almonds

Cans of tuna may be pre-chilled. Mix all ingredients well and serve on lettuce or use to stuff tomatoes; additional mayonnaise may be used but be careful not to make it too soupy. Do not prepare much in advance of serving because your tuna will darken and almonds will lose crispness. Makes 4 servings.

Restaurant Recipe

High Points Coffee & Books on the Square

125 Court Square
Ashland, AL 36251
256-354-2481

High Points Coffee & Books, owned by Melvine and Johnie Sentell, opened October 2005 in the oldest brick building on the Clay County Courthouse Square. It was built around 1900 by Dr. J.W. Jordan for his medical practice and a drugstore for his son, J. Dotson ("Dot") Jordan. Focusing on light lunches with a variety of sandwiches, soups, and salads, the menu varies a little each day. Tuna salad is a local favorite as well as Melvine's Chicken Salad which was selected as one of the "100 Dishes to Eat in Alabama Before You Die."

Wednesday – Saturday:
9:00 am to 2:00 pm

THINKSTOCK/ISTOCK

The Bright Star Restaurant

304 North 19th Street • Bessemer, AL 35020
205-424-9444 • www.thebrightstar.com

Located in historic downtown Bessemer, The Bright Star is proud to be the oldest family-owned restaurant in Alabama serving generations of guests for over 105 years. Their cuisine is best described as southern with a Greek flair, with a traditional meat-and-three offered at lunch and a variety of steaks and seafood served at dinner. The restaurant brings in fresh Gulf snapper twice weekly where it is cut in-house by staff. The Bright Star has a regional following and won the 2010 James Beard Award as an American Classic and was voted as preparing the Best Steak in Alabama by the Alabama Cattleman's Association.

LUNCH
Daily: 11:00 am to 3:00 pm
DINNER
Sunday – Thursday: 4:30 pm to 9:00 pm
Friday & Saturday: 4:30 pm to 10:00 pm

Tenderloin of Beef Greek Style

Marinade:

2 cups olive oil

⅓ cup lemon juice

1½ tablespoons minced garlic

1 teaspoon oregano

Salt and pepper to taste

4 (9- to 10-ounce) beef tenderloins, cleaned and butterflied

Combine olive oil, lemon juice, garlic, oregano, salt and pepper. Place tenderloins in marinade and refrigerate 2 to 3 hours.

Sauce:

¾ cup butter, melted

2 tablespoons lemon juice

½ tablespoon minced garlic

1 teaspoon oregano

Mix all Sauce ingredients thoroughly.

Remove tenderloins from marinade (discard marinade). Broil or charbroil tenderloins to desired temperature. Transfer to serving plate and top each with 2 ounces sauce. Serves 4.

Restaurant Recipe

Greek Style Snapper

Sauce:

Juice of 3 lemons

Oregano to taste

Salt and pepper to taste

1 cup extra virgin olive oil

Make sauce by mixing lemon juice, oregano, salt and pepper in bowl with wire whisk. Slowly add 1 cup olive oil, whisking until emulsified.

Fish:

1 stick butter, melted

6 (8-ounce) fresh snapper fillets

½ cup flour for dusting

1 teaspoon extra virgin olive oil

To prepare fish, pour melted butter over each fillet, coating evenly. Lightly dust with flour. Cook in a heavy skillet coated with 1 teaspoon olive oil or on a griddle until lightly browned. Pour sauce over grilled fish and serve immediately. Serves 6.

Restaurant Recipe

Bogue's

**3120 Clairmont Avenue South, Suite 110
Birmingham, AL 35205
205-254-9780**

Since the 1930's, Bogue's has been the favorite place for breakfast in the Birmingham area. If you visit during the week, be sure to try the homemade sweet rolls. Every day, the omelets are fluffy and perfectly cooked, the grits are creamy and perfectly seasoned, and their homemade biscuits are just like your grandma made. No matter what you order, be ready for a traditional and delicious southern breakfast. If you are coming at lunch, their meat-and-three lunch specials are sure to please everyone. At Bogue's you are treated just like family, so stop by, have a sweet roll, and enjoy the food.

**Monday – Friday: 6:00 am to 2:00 pm
Saturday: 6:00 am to 12:00 pm
Sunday: 7:00 am to 2:00 pm**

Spinach Parmesan Dip

**1 pound fresh baby spinach leaves
¾ cup sour cream
¼ cup grated Parmesan cheese
1 garlic clove, finely chopped
½ teaspoon nutmeg
1 teaspoon salt**

Steam spinach (can microwave) just until wilted, drain well and cool. Purée spinach with remaining ingredients in a blender until smooth. Serve immediately or refrigerate until ready to serve with tortilla chips for dipping.

Local Favorite

THINKSTOCK/ISTOCK

Redneck Oysters

Oysters

Minced onions

Chopped red and green peppers

Chopped ham

Shredded cheese

Place oysters on flat grill, heat them up. Remove from grill and place on a plate and top with remaining ingredients. Serve with cocktail sauce, horseradish, lemon and crackers

Restaurant Recipe

THINKSTOCK/ISTOCK/ MATHIEU BOIVIN

THINKSTOCK/ISTOCK

Courtyard Oyster Bar & Grill

4643 Highway 280, Suite M
Birmingham, AL 35242
205-980-9891

When you are ready to leave the children at home and enjoy some nighttime fun, make your way to Courtyard Oyster Bar & Grill. They have an excellent bar selection, but don't expect bar food. Their appetizers are delicious. Courtyard is the place to go for a perfectly cooked steak. If you want a cozy dinner for two with drinks, if you want to hang out with your friends and catch a game or if you are in the mood to shoot some pool after dinner, Courtyard Oyster Bar & Grill delivers.

7 days a week: 11:00 am to 5:00 am

Fife's Restaurant

2321 Fourth Avenue North
Birmingham, AL 35203
205-254-9167

Fife's Restaurant, across from the downtown Birmingham Post Office, has been the stop for breakfast, lunch, and dinner since 1955. Breakfasts of pancakes, eggs, bacon, sausage, grits, and a variety of other foods are served until 10:30 am. Lunch and dinner menus are changed daily, featuring dishes such as fried or baked chicken, spaghetti and meatballs, meatloaf, stew, steaks, and macaroni and cheese. Vegetables may include fried okra, squash, green beans, mashed potatoes, fried green tomatoes, and greens. The banana pudding and peach cobbler, warm from the oven, are delicious and crowd favorites.

Monday – Saturday: 6:00 am to 6:00 pm

Easy Peach Cobbler Recipe

½ cup real butter

1 (16-ounce) can sliced peaches

1 cup plus 2 tablespoons sugar, divided

1 cup self-rising flour

¼ teaspoon cinnamon

⅛ teaspoon nutmeg

1 cup milk (whole or 2%)

Preheat oven to 325°. Melt butter in a saucepan and then pour into an 8x8-inch baking dish to cover bottom. Add peaches (with syrup) and 2 tablespoons sugar to saucepan; bring to a boil. Remove from heat and set aside. Mix flour, 1 cup sugar, cinnamon and nutmeg in a bowl. Stir in milk just until mixture is moistened. Pour half into baking dish over butter. Pour peach slices and most of the syrup over batter. Spoon remaining batter over slices. Bake 50 to 55 minutes or until top is golden brown. Cool about 10 minutes and serve.

Family Favorite

George's BBQ Shrimp & Grits—Louisiana Style

½ cup extra virgin olive oil

3 garlic cloves, minced

1 tablespoon finely chopped rosemary

2 lemons, squeezed to make ⅓ cup juice, then sliced

¼ cup Worcestershire sauce

1½ teaspoons hot sauce or to taste

1 pound medium to large shrimp, peeled with heads (optional) and tails

1½ teaspoons Creole seasoning

½ teaspoon coarse salt

Freshly ground black pepper

Red pepper flakes to taste

Heat a 12-inch skillet (preferably cast iron) over medium heat. Add olive oil. When hot, add garlic, rosemary, lemon juice and lemon rinds. Stir in Worcestershire and hot sauce and bring to a simmer. Season shrimp with Creole seasoning, salt, pepper and red pepper. Add to skillet and cook until slightly firm to the touch. Serve shrimp on a plate with sauce over top and crusty bread on the side. Serves 4.

Restaurant Recipe

The Fish Market Restaurant

**612 22nd Street South
Birmingham, AL 35233
205-322-3330
www.thefishmarket.net**

With more than 40 years in the restaurant business, owner George Sarris welcomes you with plenty of Greek hospitality and the best fresh seafood around. State-of-the-art tanks hold a choice selection of live seafood—shrimp, blue crab, rainbow trout, tilapia, and seafood. More than 30 feet of fresh fish display cases offer up an amazing selection that will be prepared with the genuine knowledge and expertise longtime customers have come to rely on. Offering a comfortable and casual dine-in experience, expanded fresh fish and market offerings, fine foods to go, and exciting catering choices, The Fish Market will quickly become your favorite.

**Monday – Thursday: 10:00 am to 9:00 pm
Friday & Saturday: 10:00 am to 10:00 pm
Sunday: 11:00 am to 5:00 pm
SEAFOOD MARKET
Monday – Thursday: 9:00 am to 6:00 pm
Friday & Saturday: 9:00 am to 7:00 pm**

Ocean

1218 20th Street South • Birmingham, AL 35205
205-933-0999 • www.oceanbirmingham.com

Voted Best Restaurant, Best Chef, recipient of *The Wine Spectator*'s Award of Excellence for the past eight years and the winner of the AAA Four Diamond award for 2007 – 2013, Ocean offers fresh seafood in an exciting and contemporary atmosphere. The menu features fresh oysters and fish from around the world. Ocean opened in 2002, is locally owned and operated by Chef George Reis, and is located in the trendy Five Points district of Birmingham's Southside. Enjoy a casual night out with friends at the inviting and contemporary patio bar, or venture inside for some of the best seafood in town for an award-winning dining experience.

Tuesday – Saturday beginning at 5:30 pm
Reservations are accepted Tuesday through Saturday and we offer complimentary valet.

Gulf of Mexico Grilled Cobia, Chilton County Peaches, Grilled Vidalia Onion

½ cup mirin (sweetened rice wine; only 25 calories and no fat)

1 lemon, divided

Sea salt (I prefer Sel Gris from France)

Freshly cracked black pepper

4 Chilton County peaches (an Alabama favorite!), cut in half, pits removed

1 medium Vidalia onion, sliced

4 (6-ounce) Gulf Coast fresh cobia fillets

Nonstick spray, olive oil flavor

Extra virgin olive oil, for top

Blend mirin, juice of half the lemon, sea salt and cracked black pepper together. Add peaches and sliced Vidalia onion. Allow to sit 15 to 20 minutes. Preheat grill to medium-high (I prefer using a wood grill or charcoal). Season cobia with salt and pepper and spray with nonstick spray. Place on grill and cook 5 to 6 minutes per side until the cobia is cooked through. Meanwhile on a "low spot" (slightly cooler area), place Vidalia onion and peaches flesh side down on grill. Cook several minutes until well marked, turn over and cook through. Place peaches and Vidalia onion on center of the plate, top with cobia fillet, and finish with a drizzle of extra virgin olive oil and juice of remaining half the lemon. I recommend serving with a small side salad of fresh tomato and cucumber as a perfect compliment. Serves 4.

George Reis
Chef/Owner of Ocean and 26
Restaurant Recipe

Ragtime Café

2080 Valleydale Road
Birmingham, AL 35244
205-988-5323
www.ragtimecafe.com

Ragtime Café is a full-service bar and restaurant featuring all your favorite beers, wines, and mixed drinks, as well as awesome pub food and pizzas, plus seafood and steak entrées. They are open for lunch and dinner, Monday through Saturday, serving everything from satisfying appetizers to gourmet pizzas to a selection of sweet desserts. Their seafood is fresh and their high-quality steaks are grilled to order.

Ragtime Café has something to please everyone. Drop by to see why they are a neighborhood favorite.

Monday – Saturday:
11:00 am to 10:00 pm

THINKSTOCK/ISTOCK/NAOMI BASSITT

Coconut–Crusted Grouper with Vanilla Bean Cream Sauce

Grouper:

¾ cup coconut

¾ cup panko breadcrumbs

¼ cup crushed almonds

2 cups flour

2 tablespoons kosher salt

1 tablespoon black pepper

2 eggs

1 cup whole milk

1 to 4 (6-ounce) grouper fillets

6 tablespoons clarified unsalted butter

Mix coconut, breadcrumbs and almonds on baking sheet and toast in oven at 350° for approximately 5 minutes or until golden brown. Remove to a plate and set aside. Mix flour, salt and pepper and put on a plate. Beat eggs and milk together in bowl. Dip flesh side of fillet in flour, pat off; dip in egg wash and then coconut mix. In a saucepan, heat clarified butter over medium heat. Place fillet skin side up in pan and cook 3 minutes. Flip and cook 2 minutes. Finish in 350° oven for 7 minutes. Remove to a serving plate, skin side down. Pour about 2 ounces (4 tablespoons) Vanilla Bean Cream Sauce over fish fillet and serve.

Vanilla Bean Cream Sauce:

1 cup white wine

½ shallot, chopped

1 vanilla bean, cut in half lengthwise

2 cups heavy cream

1 cube fish stock

5 tablespoons cold unsalted butter, cut in pieces

½ teaspoon kosher salt

¼ teaspoon black pepper

In a saucepan, bring white wine, shallot and vanilla bean to boil. Cook about 5 to 7 minutes to reduce liquid. Add heavy cream and fish cube; bring to a boil and simmer about 4 minutes. Stir in butter until smooth; strain through a wire mesh, squeezing out all liquid. Season with salt and pepper.

Restaurant Recipe

26

1210 20th Street South • Birmingham, AL 35205
205-918-0726 • www.26twentysix.com

Brothers... Both born on the 26th, 2 years and 6 months apart.

Ocean (see page 82) gained a sibling in 2006... with the same city-feel but industrial-chic decor and the buzz of bistro dining. Slow-roasted, rustic flavors meet fast, fresh influences... Light and heavy play together with the extraordinary flavor combinations that Chef George Reis does so well.

When it opened, *26* was named "Birmingham's Best New Restaurant" by the *Birmingham News* and is the recipient of the Wine Spectator Award for the past five years. The big-city atmosphere of 26 makes it unlike any other restaurant in town. From the art deco-inspired seating, to the LED-lit bar, there's always something new to see at 26. The eclectic dishes on the menu rival those of the biggest names in food.

LUNCH: Monday – Friday: 11:00 am to 2:00 pm
DINNER:
Monday – Thursday: 5:00 pm to 10:00 pm • Friday & Saturday: 5:00 pm to 11:00 pm
Reservations are accepted Monday – Thursday for dinner and we offer complimentary valet.

Grilled Fish Reuben with Crunchy Slaw

4 (6- to 7-ounce) snapper fillets

Greek seasoning

Butter

8 slices rye bread

8 slices Dill Havarti cheese

Crunchy Slaw (recipe below)

Rémoulade (recipe below)

Season snapper fillets with Greek seasoning. Grill 2 to 3 minutes on each side. Butter bread and place 1 slice cheese on each slice; toast. Spread Rémoulade on bread. Top with Crunchy Slaw then 1 fillet. Top with another slice of bread. Yields 4 sandwiches.

Sweet Slaw Sauce:

1½ cups mayonnaise

½ cup sugar

1½ lemons, juiced

1½ limes, juiced

1½ oranges, juiced

Combine all ingredients; mix well. Refrigerate until ready to use.

Crunchy Slaw:

¼ head green cabbage

⅛ head purple cabbage

2 carrots, shredded

½ cup Sweet Slaw Sauce (recipe above)

Combine all ingredients; mix well.

Rémoulade:

½ cup mayonnaise

¼ cup ketchup

1 teaspoon whole grain mustard

Sprig of thyme

¼ teaspoon minced garlic

1 tablespoon capers

1 teaspoon dill

Combine all ingredients; mix well.

George Reis
Chef/Owner of Ocean/26
Restaurant Recipe

VULCAN STATUE
Birmingham, Alabama

The Vulcan statue located at Vulcan Park is the largest cast-iron statue in the world, but it could be called the largest "mooning" statue. The 56-foot-tall statue depicts the Roman god Vulcan, god of fire and forge, bare buttocks and all. The statue's naked buttocks have been the source of humor for many years. A novelty song, "Moon Over Homewood," refers to the fact that the statue "moons" the neighboring suburb of Homewood, Alabama. The statue was built as Birmingham's entry to the 1904 World's Fair and honors the city's history in the iron and steel industry.

For more information:
www.visitvulcan.com

Crescent Sausage Bites

1 pound ground sausage

Salt and pepper to taste

1 (8-ounce) package cream cheese, cubed

2 (8-ounce) packages crescent rolls

Preheat oven to 375°. Brown sausage with salt and pepper to taste; drain. Add cream cheese and stir until melted. Without separating them, place 1 package crescent rolls onto a baking sheet and gently press seams together to seal. Spread sausage mixture evenly over top, leaving about a ½-inch border along the edges. Unroll second package of crescent rolls and place on top. Gently press seams together. Bake about 20 minutes, or until golden brown. Cut into small squares and serve. Delicious with pizza sauce for dipping.

Local Favorite

Pizza Bar • Lacy's

141 Northwest 2nd Street
Carbon Hill, AL 35549
205-924-9316

The Pizza Bar, also known as Lacy's, a staple of the Walker County area for more than 40 years, serves up fresh, made-to-order hamburgers the way your grandma used to make along with sandwiches served on their unique New Orleans-style sub bread—a delicious garlic buttery bread that is an option on all sandwiches. You will also enjoy a wide variety of items including freshly smoked pit barbecue, fresh salads made to order, and any style of pizza you can want. Customers have been returning since 1972 because no one leaves the Pizza Bar hungry or unhappy.

Monday – Thursday: 10:00 am to 10:00 pm
Friday & Saturday: 10:00 am to 11:00 pm

Hartley's Down Home Kitchen

150 Chelsea Corners Way
Chelsea, AL 35043
205-678-4990

Satisfy your hankering for southern soul food at Hartley's Down Home Kitchen. This family-owned restaurant welcomes you with warm, down-home feel and a courteous staff. Not your average meat-and-three, they serve-up delicious homemade food cooked fresh. And if the finest soul food around isn't enough for you, their desserts will make you want to slap your momma. Their homemade peach cobbler is not to be missed. No matter what you decide to eat at Hartley's, it always tastes great and is served with a smile. Visit them today, and "Put a little Down-Home in your Day."

LUNCH
Sunday – Friday: 11:00 am to 2:00 pm
DINNER
Wednesday – Friday: 5:00 pm to 8:00 pm
Closed Saturdays

Loaded Potato Casserole

6 large baking potatoes
1 large onion
1 medium bell pepper
1 stick butter, divided
½ cup milk
½ cup mayonnaise
Salt and pepper to taste
2 cups sharp Cheddar cheese, divided
1 (8-ounce) carton sour cream
4 strips bacon, cooked and crumbled

Peel, dice and boil potatoes until fork tender. While potatoes are cooking, sauté onion and bell pepper in ½ stick butter until peppers are tender and onions are transparent. Drain potatoes; place into a mixing bowl. Add remaining ½ stick butter, milk, mayonnaise, salt and pepper. Mix well with mixer until creamy and smooth. In a casserole dish, layer ½ potato mixture. Top with sour cream, sautéed onions and peppers and 1 cup cheese. Season with salt and pepper. Top with remaining potatoes then remaining cheese. Sprinkle bacon over cheese. Cover with foil and bake at 350° for 30 minutes. Makes 6 to 8 servings good size servings.

Restaurant Recipe

Pecan Pie Recipe

½ stick margarine

1 cup sugar

½ cup Karo syrup

3 eggs, slightly beaten

1 teaspoon vanilla extract

1 cup pecans

1 (9-inch) pie shell

Melt margarine in a saucepan over medium heat; add sugar and Karo. Remove from heat. Add a small amount to eggs then return egg mixture to sugar mixture. Stir until well mixed. Add pecans and vanilla; pour mixture into pie shell. Bake at 325° for 1 hour. Cool before cutting as pie will harden as it cools.

Restaurant Recipe

HEATON Pecan FARM

Homemade Pecan Candies, Pies, Cakes, Pecan Butter, Jam
Sixteen Flavors of Gourmet Ice Cream, Gift Loft and Deli

I-65 - Exit 208	Phone: 1-205-755-8654
309 Sunrise Boulevard	Toll Free: 1-800-446-3531
Clanton, Alabama 35045	HeatonPecanFarm@BellSouth.net

In 1962 John & Billie Heaton purchased a grove of large, bountiful pecan trees that were planted as far back as 1919. One year later, they were in the pecan business, marketing whole pecans directly to their customers. In 1990, they opened The Barn, where you'll find unique pecan treats, an ice cream counter featuring 16 flavors of homemade ice cream (10 include pecans), and a flavorful breakfast and lunch menu, including a full-service deli. Nearly every treat in the store is hand-made fresh each day. Quality and customer service are the main ingredients at Heaton Pecan Farm.

**Monday – Thursday:
9:00 am to 5:00 pm**

**Friday – Sunday:
9:00 am to 6:00 pm**

www.HEATON.com

Main Street Café

**613A 2nd Avenue North
Clanton, AL 35045
205-755-2216**

Main Street Café is like eating at Mama's house. If you are in the mood for great country cooking, this is the place to be. You'll find a packed house for breakfast and lunch because the food is so good. Just go ahead and squeeze in; you won't regret it. For breakfast, they have hands-down the best pancakes around plus all the great breakfast standards. For lunch, this is not just your average meat-and-three. You will enjoy delicious southern-style cooking with exceptional quality and taste, served up with a smile and a generous amount of southern hospitality.

Call for hours

Broccoli Casserole

1 (32-ounce) package frozen broccoli spears

1 cup diced onion

1½ sticks margarine, divided

1 (10-ounce) can cream of mushroom soup

4 tablespoons mayonnaise

½ teaspoon black pepper

½ teaspoon salt

2 cups shredded mild Cheddar cheese

2 sleeves snack crackers, crumbled

Steam broccoli until tender; drain water and set aside. Sauté onions in ¾ stick margarine. In a bowl, combine soup, mayonnaise, salt and pepper. Add sautéed onions with their butter. Mix together until blended. In 9x13-inch pan, layer broccoli, soup mixture, cheese and crackers in that order. Melt remaining ¾ stick margarine and drizzle over crackers. Bake at 375° for 30 minutes.

Restaurant Recipe

BIG PEACH WATER TOWER

Clanton, Alabama

When you see their local water tower, you don't have to wonder about Chilton County's claim to fame—Alabama's largest producer of peaches. The water tower, which is 120 feet tall and holds 500,000 gallons of water, looks like a giant peach.

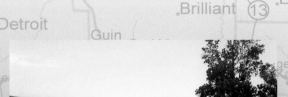

Fresh Peach Ice Cream

4 cups sliced peaches

3 cups sugar, divided

1 quart (4 cups) heavy cream

1 quart (4 cups) milk

**1 (14-ounce) can sweetened
condensed milk**

1½ cups sugar

1 teaspoon vanilla extract

½ teaspoon almond extract

4 pasteurized eggs

Combine peaches with 1½ cups sugar;
set aside. Combine cream, milk and
condensed milk. Stir in 1½ cups sugar,
extracts and eggs. Add peaches and
stir well. Place in ice cream freezer and
freeze per freezer directions.

Family Favorite

Peach Park

**Located I-65 Exit 205
2300 7th Street South
Clanton, AL 35046
205-755-2065**

Gene and Francis Gray opened Peach
Park as a produce and ice cream business
in 1984. It since has grown to include
serving fresh peach, strawberry, and
blackberry cobblers. Peach Park has fried
pies, sandwiches, salads, cakes and has an
in-season fresh fruit bar.

And yes it does have a park, complete
with a children's playground and RV
parking. YA'LL COME !!

**Open March thru November
7 days a week: 8:00 am to 8:00 pm
Extended hours in summer**

Peach Cobbler

Filling:

4 cups peeled and sliced peaches

3 cups sugar, divided

¼ cup butter, melted

1½ tablespoons Sure-Gel fruit pectin

1½ tablespoons peach gelatin

2 teaspoons vanilla extract

Place peaches in a bowl with 1½ cups sugar and melted butter. Mix remaining sugar with fruit pectin, peach gelatin and vanilla. Add to peaches and stir.

Pastry:

⅔ cup shortening

½ teaspoon salt

2 cups plain flour

2 teaspoons almond extract

Boil ⅓ cup water. Add shortening and salt; remove from heat. Stir in flour and almond extract with a fork until dough holds together. Remove from pan, split into two even balls. Place one on a piece of wax paper and the other in a bowl to keep warm. Place another piece of wax paper over dough and roll to ⅛ inch thick. Place on treated baking sheet and bake at 325° until dry but not browned. Crumble baked crust into the bottom of a pie plate or casserole dish.

To finish:

½ stick butter

1 egg white, beaten

2 tablespoons sugar

Pour peach filling over crumbs, dot with butter. Roll reserved crust between two pieces of wax paper. Place over peaches, brush with egg white, sprinkle with sugar and cut slits in crust. Bake 25 minutes or until lightly browned.

Family Favorite

Red's Catfish Cabin

689 Catfish Road
Cragford, AL
256-354-7705
www.redscatfish.com

Red's Catfish Cabin sits atop a knoll overlooking Elbert "Red" Kennedy's 11 acres of fish pond, surrounded by open pastures and adjoining woodlands. The two-story building, constructed mainly of rough pine lumber cut from Kennedy's farm, has more than 7,000 feet of floor space. From day one it's been a success. Open only Thursday through Sunday, Red's serves about 1,200 pounds of catfish each week. From the tranquility of the rural setting to the rustic building, the relaxed down-home atmosphere to the friendly staff, there's just something about the place. Visit them to experience it for yourself.

Thursday: 4:00 pm to 8:00 pm
Friday: 3:00 pm to 9:00 pm
Saturday: 11:00 am to 9:00 pm
Sunday: 11:00 am to 3:00 pm

Butter Roll

Larry's grandmother made this for him when he was a child.

Biscuit dough using your favorite recipe (for about 9 biscuits)

1 pint (2 cups) whole milk

½ teaspoon vanilla extract

1 stick butter (real butter is best), softened

½ cup sugar plus more for topping

Roll biscuit dough flat and cut in half. Place each piece side-by-side in bottom of a 9x13-inch baking pan. Combine milk, vanilla, butter and ½ cup sugar; pour over biscuit dough. Bake at 350° about 40 minutes or until just before done. Remove from oven and sprinkle additional sugar over top; return to oven to brown. As a variation, add your favorite fruit to make it a fruit cobbler.

Restaurant Recipe

Leo & Susie's Famous Green Top Bar-B-Q

**7530 Highway 78
Dora, AL 35062
205-648-9838
www.greentopbbq.com**

Why has the Green Top has been around since Truman was in the White House? Because they serve some of the best barbecue on the planet. An Alabama icon, their menu has a little something for everyone—barbecue pork sandwiches, barbecue plates, barbecue potatoes, and even barbecue salads. If barbecue is not your thing, they offer chef and tossed salads, hamburgers, and chopped chicken sandwiches. Their home fries are a local favorite. Leo & Susie's Famous Green Top is family friendly so the next time you have a cravin' for something really good, stop by. They'll "keep the hickory fire burning for you."

**Monday – Wednesday: 8:30 am to 9:00 pm
Thursday – Saturday: 8:30 am to 10:00 pm**

Green Top's Baked Beans

**1 pound bacon, cut in 1-inch cubes
1 small onion, diced
1 bell pepper, sliced
2 (15-ounce) cans pork and beans
½ cup dark corn syrup
4 cups Green Top Bar-B-Que Sauce**

Preheat oven to 350°. Sauté bacon, onion and bell pepper in a skillet until bacon is done. In a baking dish, combine beans, bacon mixture, syrup and barbecue sauce. Bake 45 minutes.

Restaurant Recipe

LALA'S PLACE

3004 County Road 44
Eldridge, AL 35554
205-487-0315

Welcome to LALA'S PLACE, home of the biggest, "baddest" burger around. LALA'S is a quaint, little, out-of-the-way place reminiscent of days gone by when people practiced the idea that the customer is always right. In business since 2008, they feature a first, second, and third generation of family cooks. The restaurant is a little out of the way, but worth the drive. All items are cooked to order. Call ahead and they'll have it ready.

Monday – Saturday:
11:00 am to 2:00 pm
and
4:30 pm until...

Mother's Family Slaw

1 medium head cabbage
1 medium yellow onion
1 small carrot
¼ cup sugar
1 tablespoon salt
2 tablespoons white vinegar
1 cup mayonnaise
2 shakes Mrs. Dash Original Seasoning

Grate cabbage, onion and carrot on medium side of grater into medium mixing bowl. Add sugar and stir well with fork. Add salt and vinegar; mix well again. Add mayonnaise and mix well. Place in refrigerator for ½ to 1 hour. Remove from refrigerator and mix well. Taste to see if slaw needs a little bit more sugar or vinegar. Just before serving, sprinkle with Mrs. Dash.

Restaurant Recipe

Cornbread Salad

This recipe is great for leftover cornbread. It is one of the favorites in the restaurant.

6 cups crumbled cornbread

½ cup diced green pepper

½ cup whole-kernel corn (no juice)

1 cup diced fresh tomatoes

1 small onion, diced

½ cup bacon bits

⅛ teaspoon rubbed sage

Salt and pepper to taste

Mayonnaise to moisten

Combine all ingredients using just enough mayonnaise to hold mixture together well or to your taste.

Restaurant Recipe

Sweet Digs

310 Court Street • Fayette, AL 35555
www.lunchatsweetdigs.blogspot.com
205-270-0794

Sweet Digs, located in downtown Fayette, specializes in southern cuisine. Their menu changes daily and offers a choice of at least two meats, a variety of veggies and casseroles, fresh homemade yeast rolls, and yummy desserts. If the hot plate is not your thing, try their chicken salad—it's a local favorite. Many have said, "It is like going home for Sunday lunch." So, if you want some delicious home-style cooking, visit Sweet Digs. But go early... some days the specials don't last too long.

Monday – Thursday: 11:00 am to 2:00 pm

Beans and Greens

10294 Centre Road
Gadsden, AL 35903
256-492-3267

8314 Alabama Highway 144
Alexandria, AL 36250
256-770-7235
www.beansandgreensllc.com

Owners Bobby and Kelly Boles have been serving up yummy, favorite southern dishes like your grandma makes for the last twelve years. Beans and Greens' secret southern recipes have been passed down generation after generation. Today, their made-from-scratch recipes, including world famous hand-breaded chicken fingers and banana pudding, have become southern popular favorites. At Beans and Greens, the mission is to make our customers feel happy and their bellies full by providing a family-style dining experience with a buffet full of delicious southern classics. There is a touch of granny's love in every bite that will leave your mouth watering for more.

Monday – Thursday: 7:00 am to 8:30 pm
Friday & Saturday: 7:00 am to 9:00 pm
Sunday: 7:00 am to 3:00 pm

The Perfect Meatloaf

10 pounds ground hamburger

1 cup chopped onion

1 cup chopped bell pepper

2 eggs, beaten

¼ cup Worcestershire sauce

1 cup ketchup

1 cup sweetened condensed milk

2 cups crushed saltine crackers

Salt, black pepper, onion powder and garlic powder to taste

In a large bowl, mix all ingredients thoroughly. Set aside while oven preheats to 400°. Spray a 9x20-inch casserole dish with nonstick cooking spray. Form mixture into casserole dish and cook 90 minutes, or until no longer pink in the middle. Drain excess grease.

Red Sauce:

4½ cups ketchup

2 dashes Worcestershire sauce

1 teaspoon onion powder

1 teaspoon garlic powder

1 cup brown sugar

Mix together and spread generously over meatloaf. Return to oven for 5 to 10 minutes. Cool before cutting into squares. Serve with your favorite sides. Enjoy. Makes 20 to 30 servings.

Restaurant Recipe

Poppy Seed Chicken Casserole

4 to 5 chicken breasts

1 (8-ounce) carton sour cream

2 (10-ounce) cans cream of chicken soup

3 tablespoons poppy seeds

2 cups shredded Monterey Jack cheese

1 roll Ritz crackers, crushed

Cook chicken breasts in water to cover until tender. Cool; chop into small pieces. Combine sour cream, soup and 1 can water until blended; cook over medium heat until hot. Remove from heat and add poppy seeds. Stir in cooked chicken. Add cheese and crackers; stir gently. Pour into a 9x13-inch dish and bake at 350° for approximately 25 minutes. Remove from oven and allow to set for about 15 to 20 minutes. Serve over prepared white rice.

Tammy Harvey
Family Favorite

The Coffee Well

A modern day gathering place.

124 Court Street #101
Gadsden, AL 35901
256-547-4446
www.thecoffeewell.net

The Coffee Well is a modern-day gathering place, locally owned and operated since November 2009. It is located in historic and beautiful downtown Gadsden. Don't let the name fool you, they do more than coffee well! They offer a wide selection of specialty coffee drinks—hot, iced or frozen—plus fresh-squeezed lemonade, breakfast scones, croissants, and more. Order a panini or from the full lunch menu which includes fresh, made to order salads, sandwiches, and homemade desserts. Space is available for private parties and events.

Monday – Friday: 7:30 am to 6:00 pm
Saturday: 10:00 am to 3:00 pm

Top O' the River

1606 Rainbow Drive • Gadsden, AL 35901
256-547-9817
www.topotheriverrestaurant.com

Additional locations in Lake Guntersville and Anniston

Top O' the River has been open for over 30 years and is family owned and operated. All locations specialize in catfish, seafood, steaks, and chicken, and proudly serve only USA farm-raised catfish from Mississippi. Don't forget to also order their famous mustard greens, fried pickles, and onion rings. Top O' the River takes pride in serving their customers. You can expect friendly service and a comfortable atmosphere. Each Alabama location has the capacity to seat up to 600 customers. They can also accommodate large parties in banquet rooms that can seat up to 50 people.

Monday – Thursday: 5:00 pm to 9:00 pm
Friday: 5:00 pm to 10:00 pm
Saturday: 4:00 pm to 10:00 pm
Sunday: Noon to 8:00 pm

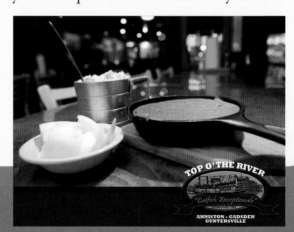

Tre Ragazzi's

Chicken Piccata

1 chicken breast, pounded and breaded

2 tablespoons butter

1 tablespoon capers

3 tablespoons lemon juice

3 tablespoons white wine

Sear chicken breast in butter until brown. Add capers, lemon juice and white wine. Cook until chicken is done and liquid has reduced to a nice sauce, about 8 minutes. Place chicken on plate with sauce. Serve with linguine on the side topped with grated pecorino cheese. Add a slice of lemon and wedge of tomato for color.

Restaurant Recipe

Tre Ragazzi's Italian Café

519 Broad Street
Gadsden, AL 35901
256-543-2726

Kevin and Toni Napper's love of Italian food began years ago after owning a small pizza place, and then when Kevin took a job selling Italian food. After a 20-year break from the restaurant business, they are back in the business, this time including their three boys. Hence the name of the business—"tre ragazzi" is Italian for three boys. It is a family affair no doubt. On the menu are authentic Italian dishes as well as stone-baked pizzas. A local favorite is the Chicken Piccata. Tre Ragazzi's slogan is "food so good you can't fugetaboutit." It is loved by the locals and you will love it too.

Monday – Thursday: 11:00 am to 9:00 pm
Friday & Saturday: 11:00 am to 10:00 pm
Sunday: 11:00 am to 2:00 pm

Ms. Kitty's Country Kitchen

18 Old Providence Road
Goodwater, AL 35072
256-329-3111

Knowing it has always been her dream, Kitty's husband surprised her with a restaurant for her 50th birthday. Since opening April 2010, Ms. Kitty's has served the community and guests from all around the state and out of state as well. Kitty says, "We recognize that God gave us this restaurant and we want to honor Him in all that we do." Ms. Kitty's menu offers a variety of foods that are always prepared fresh—nothing is ever pre-cooked. You'll feel right at home in their comfortable and friendly environment where they treat you like family.

Tuesday – Friday: 8:00 am to 8:00 pm
Saturday: 5:00 am to 8:00 pm

Lasagna Special

½ medium onion, diced
½ green bell pepper, diced
1 garlic clove, minced
2 teaspoons olive oil
1 pound ground beef
Salt, pepper and garlic powder to taste
1 (14-ounce) can crushed tomatoes
1 (6-ounce) can tomato paste

Saute onion, bell pepper and garlic in olive oil until soft. Add ground beef; cook until done. Season to taste; add tomatoes with 1 can water and tomato paste. Simmer.

3 eggs, beaten
1 cup shredded mozzarella cheese
1 (16-ounce) container ricotta cheese
1 (4-ounce) container cottage cheese

Combine filling ingredients; mix well.

9 dry lasagna noodles
1 cup shredded mozzarella

Boil noodles until done, drain and rinse with cold water until cooled. Spread a little sauce in casserole pan. Layer 3 noodles, one third cheese filling, then one third remaining sauce. Repeat layers twice. Top with mozzarella. Bake at 350° for 30 minutes or until bubbly. Remove from oven and rest 30 minutes before cutting.

Restaurant Recipe

Super Easy Fantastic Fudge

3½ cups powdered sugar

¼ cup evaporated milk

½ cup butter

3 tablespoons cocoa

1 teaspoon vanilla extract

Put all ingredients in a microwave-safe bowl. Microwave on high for 2½ minutes; stir. Microwave another 2½ minutes. Pour on buttered plate and cool about 30 minutes.

Local Favorite

Mustang

2205 West Main Street
Greensboro, AL 36744
334-624-9301

Obscurely located in a convenience store that also doubles as a grocery store, is one of the best restaurants in the area. The restaurant at the back of Mustang Oil serves up breakfast, lunch, and dinner to locals and visitors in its friendly, casual style. You will love their delicious barbecue or fried catfish with tasty sides like potato salad, fried okra, coleslaw, and Cajun fries. A local favorite is their barbecued chicken which is moist and sweet, barbecued ribs, and their hot, crunchy sweet potato fries.

Monday – Wednesday: 4:00 am to 4:30 pm
Thursday – Saturday: 4:00 am to 9:00 pm

Savage's Bakery

2916 18th Street South
Homewood, AL 35209
205-871-4901
www.savagebakery.com

Savage's Bakery has been a Birmingham landmark for more than 70 years. Established in 1939, the bakery was purchased in 1978 by Van Scott, who still owns and operates the bakery. A true family-owned and operated business, at Savage's everyone "knows your name." They are "famous" for smiley-face cookies, roulage, meltaways, petit-fours, butterflake rolls and, of course, their CAKES. There is also a made-to-order deli that is known for the Reuben sandwich, baked ham & cheese biscuits, chicken salad, and the pimento cheese which was voted "Top 100 Things You Must Eat Before You Die."

Monday – Friday: 8:00 am to 5:30 pm
Saturday: 9:00 am to 5:00 pm • Sunday: CLOSED

Cheese Cookies

I highly recommend this recipe. My great-grandmother used to make these all the time, therefore my dad (Van Scott) grew up eating them. They are technically a cheese straw, but have always been called Cheese Cookies.

½ pound sharp Cheddar cheese, grated

½ pound butter, softened

2 cups flour

2½ cups Rice Krispies

½ teaspoon cayenne pepper

Mix cheese and butter. With your hands mix in remaining ingredients until uniformly mixed. Roll into walnut-sized balls. Flatten each a little and place on a lightly greased baking sheet. Bake at 350° for 15 minutes. Cool on racks. Store in fridge or freeze. From fridge, reheat to 400° for 5 to 7 minutes. If frozen, defrost in fridge before reheating.

Family Favorite

3043 Allison Bonnett Memorial Drive
Hueytown, AL 35023
205-491-1333
www.unclesamsbbq.com

Uncle Sam's Wants You... to enjoy their outstanding barbecue. And you won't be disappointed because you get a lot for what you pay. From the outside, Uncle Sam's looks like your typical small-town barbecue joint. The tremendous smell coming from their open pit barbecue will quickly let you know that this is above standard barbecue with a delicious balance of smoke flavor. You'll find pork, beef, chicken and ribs in a tasty, sweet, wet barbecue sauce along with great snacks like chicken fingers, jumbo baked potatoes, and barbecue salad. Sides include beans, slaw, red potato salad, and homemade onion rings. Their lunch specials are super-popular and if you need to feed the family, try their family-size take-out deals.

7 days a week: 10 am to 8 pm
Drive-thru: 10 am to 9 pm

Brunswick Stew

1 pound pulled chicken
1 pound barbecued pork

Meat should be cooked outside on grill.

1 tablespoon salt
½ tablespoon black pepper
2 to 3 onions, chopped
2 cups ketchup
1 teaspoon dry mustard
½ cup Worcestershire sauce
2 tablespoons hot sauce
2 (28-ounce) cans diced tomatoes
**2 (16-ounce) cans yellow
cream-style corn**
2 (16-ounce) cans lima beans, drained
3 tablespoons white vinegar
1 (16-ounce) can okra

Put chicken, pork, salt and pepper in a large pot. Add 8 cups water and remaining ingredients, except okra. Bring to a boil. Reduce heat to a simmer, cover and simmer 2 hours. Add okra; simmer another 20 minutes. Can be served immediately, but the longer it sits the better is gets. It's best 2 to 3 days later.

Family Favorite

Tuna Salad

1 (66-ounce) can Starkist tuna

4 boiled eggs, chopped

3 stalks celery, diced small

3 tablespoons sweet relish

3 tablespoons jalapeño juice

White pepper to taste

3 to 4 tablespoons mayonnaise
or more to taste

Mix ingredients well. Refrigerate.

Bowl of Chili

5 pounds ground chuck

1 small yellow onion, chopped

3 tablespoons chili powder

3 tablespoons ground cumin

Dash red pepper to taste

2 (15-ounce) cans Hunt's
Dinner Starters seasoned tomato
sauce for chili

3 (27-ounce) cans Bush's Best
chili beans in mild sauce

1 (15-ounce) can black beans

1 (15-ounce) can dark red
kidney beans

Sauté meat and onions; drain grease.
Add spices and stir well. Add tomatoes
and beans. Cook low and slow until
it boils. Continue to cook 1 hour or
longer. Add water as needed.

Restaurant Recipe

Gus' Hot Dogs

**5415 Beacon Drive, Suite 139
Irondale, AL 35210
205-956-6622
www.gushotdogs.com**

Gus' Hot Dogs in Irondale has been
serving delicious food for more than 22
years. John Musso, the owner since June
2001, says that his restaurant traces its roots
directly back to the original Gus' opened
in 1947 in downtown Birmingham by
Gus Alexander. Those original recipes are
still made fresh daily and have become
local favorites. They include hot dog
sauce, chili, hot beef and slaw. Added
along the way have been homemade
chicken and tuna salad, pimiento cheese,
and a seasonal bowl of chili. At Gus' they
pay attention to detail. From fry salt to
tea brewing, special seasoned hand patted
burgers and freshly prepared toppings,
there is something on the menu for
everyone. You will experience a unique
and tasty dining experience. Stop by and
visit as you travel across Alabama.

**Monday – Friday: 10:30 am to 4:00 pm
Saturday: 10:30 am to 3:00 pm**

Cooter Brown's Rib Shack

8464 Alabama Highway 204
Jacksonville, AL 36265
256-435-1514
www.cootersribs.com

Cooter Brown's Rib Shack is a family-owned and operated full-service restaurant. From the outside, the place still looks like a county line beer joint. Once inside, however, you'll find a cozy, relaxing atmosphere with a friendly staff eager to serve you. If you are in the area, drop in and taste why their ribs are listed as one of the "100 Dishes to Eat in Alabama Before You Die" by the Alabama Board of Tourism. Just remember, their food is as good as their building is ugly. Cooter Brown's Rib Shack, home of Good Ribs & Tasty Butts.

Monday – Wednesday:
4:00 pm to 9:00 pm
Thursday – Saturday:
11:00 am to 10:00 pm

Down South Philly Sandwich

2 slices Texas toast

Sliced onions

Sliced bell peppers

1 tablespoon vegetable oil

Garlic salt and black pepper to taste

Swiss cheese

Chopped smoked pork

Cooter Brown's BBQ Sauce

Toast the bread. Sauté onions and bell peppers in oil with garlic salt and black pepper. Layer one slice of Texas toast with Swiss cheese then chopped pork. Top with onions and bell peppers. Finish with barbecue sauce and top with second slice of toast. Enjoy!

Restaurant Recipe

NOCCALULA FALLS
Gadsden, Alabama

Noccalula Falls in Gadsden is named for the lovely and kind-hearted Princess Noccalula who defied her father in a leap from the falls. Noccalula's love was young brave of her own tribe. As a great Indian chief, Noccalula's father had promised her to the rich chief of a neighboring tribe. On her wedding day, dressed in festive wedding robes, Noccalula walked away from the great wedding feast and, overcome with grief over the looming marriage, jumped to her death.

Visit www.cityofgadsden.com for more information.

Black Rock Bistro

313 19th Street West
Jasper, AL 35501
205-387-0282
www.blackrockbistro.com

Black Rock Bistro is Jasper's premier bistro, featuring dine-in and take-out for lunch and dinner. Their menu has a broad range of options, so there is something for everybody. The menu rotates between excellent lunch selections like Gulf lump crab cakes, smoked chicken salad, Creole chicken tenders, fried Apalachicola oysters, and much more. The dinner menu, which changes each Thursday and Friday night, features grilled or blackened Gulf shrimp, cornmeal-crusted Delta catfish, heritage-bred pork chops, and hand-cut rib-eyes and New York strips. The local favorite is their Catfish Pontchartrain, the restaurant's signature dish, featuring a breaded catfish fillet stuffed with Gulf shrimp and Breaux Bridge andouille sausage and finished with a Creole pan sauce.

LUNCH: Tuesday – Friday: 11:00 am to 2:00 pm
DINNER: Thursday & Friday: 5:30 pm to 9:30 pm

"With its deep Southern roots and propensity for Cajun and Creole traditions, Black Rock has a long-standing reputation as one of the premier restaurants in all of Alabama."

—*New York Magazine*

Jasper Pear–Apple Crisp

3 Golden Delicious apples, peeled, cored and thin sliced

3 medium-size Bartlett or D'Anjou pears

⅓ cup orange juice

¼ cup sugar

½ cup firmly packed light brown sugar

1½ teaspoons ground cinnamon

¼ teaspoon ground nutmeg, optional

¼ teaspoon salt

¾ cup all-purpose flour

¼ cup cold butter

Preheat oven to 375°. Butter a 9-inch square baking dish. Layer apple and pear slices in bottom. In a small bowl, combine orange juice and sugar; pour over fruit. In another bowl, mix brown sugar, cinnamon, nutmeg, salt and flour until well combined. Cut butter into mixture until it resembles coarse meal. Sprinkle evenly over fruit. Bake about 40 minutes or until topping is brown and is tender when pierced with fork. Serves 6 to 8.

Local Favorite

THINKSTOCK/ISTOCK/DUHA127

Victoria's Restaurant

1303 Highway 78 West
Jasper, AL 35501
205-384-3463
www.victoriasgiftshoponline.com

Victoria's Restaurant is a super-fun, unique place to eat and shop. The food is all made from scratch and served cafeteria-style featuring delicious meats, fresh vegetables, sweet tea, and homemade yeast rolls. What makes this restaurant so unique? There is not only an on-site bakery, but also a ladies' boutique to satisfy your mood for shopping. For more than 20 years, Victoria's Restaurant has been serving delicious home-cooked meals and their famous homemade desserts. Stop in for a great meal and you will also find the most unique fashions, clothes, and jewelry anywhere around.

Monday – Friday: 10:30 am to 7:30 pm
Saturday – Sunday: 10:30 am to 2:00 pm

Cabbage Patch Stew & Dumplings

1 pound ground beef

2 medium onions, thinly sliced

1½ cups coarsely chopped cabbage

½ cup chopped celery

1 (16-ounce) can stewed tomatoes

1 (15.5-ounce) can kidney beans

1 cup water

1 teaspoon salt

½ teaspoon pepper

1 to 2 teaspoons chili powder

2 cups Bisquick baking mix

½ cup milk

Brown ground beef in a Dutch oven or large pot; drain. Add onions, cabbage and celery; cook until vegetables are soft. Stir in tomatoes, kidney beans (with liquid), water, salt, pepper and chili powder. Bring to a boil. While waiting for stew to boil, stir baking mix and milk together to form a soft dough. Drop by spoonfuls into boiling stew. Reduce heat to simmer and cook uncovered for 10 minutes. Cover and cook an additional 10 minutes. Serves 4 to 6.

Local Favorite

New Orleans Bread Pudding

1 loaf French bread

5 cups milk

2½ cups sugar

4 eggs, beaten

½ teaspoon cinnamon

½ teaspoon vanilla extract

½ cup raisins

1 cup diced peaches

Tear French bread into pieces and place in a large mixing bowl. Pour in milk and let soak for 20 minutes. Add sugar, eggs, cinnamon and vanilla; stir well. Once mixed, add raisins and peaches and stir again. Pour completed mixture into a well-greased 9x13-inch pan and bake at 375° for 45 minutes.

Iced Topping:

3 tablespoons milk (more if needed)

1¼ cups powdered sugar

Mix milk into sugar. Add more milk, 1 tablespoon at a time, if needed to achieve desired consistency. Drizzle over bread pudding once baked.

Restaurant Recipe

Rick's Crossroads Grille

**48278 Highway 78
Lincoln, AL 35096
205-763-7266**

Rick and Jean Seal and daughter, Emily Duke, bring original New Orleans flavor to hungry diners in the Lincoln area. Located on the hill at the crossroads of Highway 77 and Highway 78, they prepare delicious Crescent City originals like red beans and rice, po' boy sandwiches, boudin, shrimp gumbo, barbecue shrimp, and Cajun grilled shrimp along with great hand-cut Angus rib-eyes, prime rib, Philly cheese steak, and some of the best fried seafood anywhere—just ask their customers. Italian dishes are also on the menu with dishes like chicken or shrimp Alfredo, spaghetti and meatballs, and tiger tilapia. Reservations are accepted.

**Monday – Thursday: 11:00 am to 8:30 pm
Friday: 11:00 am to 9:00 pm
Saturday: 3:00 pm to 9:00 pm**

Local Color Café

**5811 US Highway 11
Springville, AL 35146
205-467-0334
www.localcolorcafe.com**

For ten years, Local Color Café has been a well-kept secret haven for really good music with a supper club atmosphere. Patrons are treated to everything from smooth jazz to toe-tapping bluegrass by the best musicians in the area. Food choices are cooked fresh incorporating fresh produce from the area. Cajun and Creole dishes abound as well as good ol' southern favorites such as chicken dumplings. The smell of homemade southern-style cornbread will make your mouth water. Try the chocolate pudding cake for the perfect end to your meal. If you are looking for something a little different, check out this intimate, cozy little spot.

**Friday and Saturday nights:
6:30 pm until the music ends
Occasional Thursday night specials and
Sunday concerts
Advance reservations strongly
recommended due to limited seating.**

Local Color Cabbage Casserole

Our most requested recipe.

**8 cups cabbage, washed and
cut in pieces**

1 white onion, washed and chopped

1 teaspoon salt

**1 (10.75-ounce) can cream of
celery soup***

1½ cups mayonnaise

1½ cups shredded Cheddar cheese

1 sleeve Ritz crackers, crushed

½ stick butter or margarine, melted

Place cabbage and onion in large boiler and cover with water. Add salt, and cook until fork tender. Remove from heat and drain. In a large mixing bowl, combine cabbage and onion with soup, mayonnaise and cheese; mix thoroughly. Place mixture in a 9x13-inch greased baking pan. Top with crackers and drizzle with melted butter. Bake at 350° about 20 to 25 minutes until bubbly and cheese is melted.

Note: You may substitute any variety of creamy soup such as chicken, broccoli or asparagus with equal success.

Restaurant Recipe

Grapes in a Cloud
(Grape Salad)

4 cups red seedless grapes

4 cups green seedless grapes

1 (8-ounce) package cream cheese, softened

1 (8-ounce) carton sour cream

½ teaspoon vanilla extract

½ teaspoon almond extract

1 cup chopped pecans

½ cup brown sugar

Wash grapes and set aside. Combine cream cheese, sour cream, vanilla and almond extract. Gently fold in grapes. Refrigerate 2 hours. Stir in pecans and brown sugar. Refrigerate until ready to serve. Absolutely delicious.

Restaurant Recipe

Chocolate Puddin' Cake

3 cups all-purpose flour

3 teaspoons baking soda

1 teaspoon salt

1 cup sugar

1 cup cocoa, divided

¼ cup melted butter or margarine

1 (12-ounce) can evaporated milk

1 cup firmly packed brown sugar

4 cups hot water or use brewed coffee for richer taste

In large mixing bowl, combine flour, baking soda, salt, sugar and ½ cup cocoa. Add butter and milk; mix just until batter resembles a thick brownie dough. Spread in an ungreased 9x13-inch pan. Sprinkle 1 cup brown sugar and remaining ½ cup cocoa over batter. Gently pour water or coffee over top. Bake at 350° for approximately 30 minutes or until top is springy. Allow to rest 30 minutes or longer before serving. Scoop servings into individual dessert dishes. We top it with whipped cream and a cherry. Delicious.

Restaurant Recipe

Dreamland Bar-B-Q

1-800-752-0544
www.dreamlandbbq.com

In 1958 John "Big Daddy" Bishop opened Dreamland Café in the Jerusalem Heights Neighborhood of Tuscaloosa, Alabama. In the beginning, he and his wife Miss Lily sold everything from postage stamps to sandwiches, but one item soon out-shined the rest: the ribs. He spent countless hours perfecting his sauce and signature style for ribs and word began to spread. People

traveled from around the country to try his legendary hickory-grilled ribs and southern-style sauce. Over half-a-century later, his recipes and ribs remain unchanged and Mr. Bishop's dream is available at 7 restaurant locations across Alabama and in Atlanta. Stop by any Dreamland Bar-B-Que and find out why there "Ain't nothing like 'em nowhere!"

SEVEN LOCATIONS:

The Original Dreamland Café
5535 15th Avenue East
Tuscaloosa, AL 35405

Birmingham Dreamland
1427 14th Avenue South
Birmingham, AL 35205

Huntsville Dreamland
3855 University Drive
Huntsville, AL 35816

Roswell Dreamland
10730 Alpharetta Highway
Roswell, GA 30076

Northport Dreamland
101 Bridge Avenue
Northport, AL 35476

Montgomery Dreamland
101 Tallapoosa Street
Montgomery, AL 36104

Mobile Dreamland
3314 Old Shell Road
Mobile, AL 36607

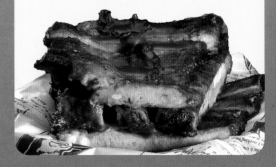

Dreamland Ships Anywhere in the Nation!

Dreamland Bar-B-Que ships their legendary BBQ ribs, pork, chicken, sausage and sauce to Anywhere, USA! You can get their mouth-watering, hickory-grilled flavor delivered right  to your doorstep. With southern sides and desserts, you'll get a taste of true Alabama tradition!

Make Dreamland's flavor your secret ingredient with their signature sauces and seasonings! Their Bar-B-Que Sauce, Dipping Sauce, Bar-B-Que Rub and Bar-B-Que Shake will have your guests beggin' for your recipe.

Check out the recipe to the right or visit the Dreamland Kitchen at **www. dreamlandbbq.com** for more ideas to make sure your meals "ain't nothing like 'em nowhere!"

BBQ Ham Shooter Sandwich

Shooter sandwiches are believed to be of British origin and are perfect for hunters out for the day. They are wrapped in butcher paper, tied with twine, and served at room temperature. We've taken the shooter sandwich style and fused it with a Philadelphia style BBQ Ham Sandwich with southern roots (i.e. Wickles from Dadeville, AL).

2 tablespoons oil

¾ cup julienned red onion

3 cups cubed hickory smoked ham

1½ teaspoons Dreamland Shake

¾ cup quartered Wickles Pickles

1 cup Dreamland Bar-B-Que Sauce

4 (6-inch) crusty hoagie buns, sliced ¾ horizontally, hollowed out

In a large sauté pan, heat oil over medium-high heat. Add onion and cook 3 minutes until soft. Stir in cubed ham and season with Dreamland Shake. Add Wickles and Dreamland Bar-B-Que Sauce, stirring to combine. Reduce heat to simmer and cook an additional 2 minutes.

Heat a clean skillet over medium high-heat. Fill each hoagie bun with 1 cup ham filling ensuring bun encloses all of the filling. (Remove any excess.) Place hoagies in hot pan and press down with a press or another pan briefly. Flip over and press again. Repeat with all sandwiches. To serve, slice horizontally. Serves 4.

Family Favorite

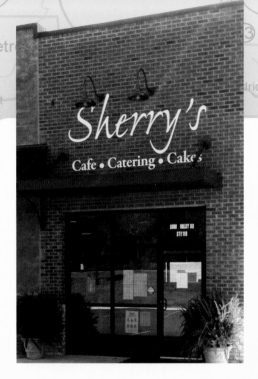

Sherry's Café & Catering

5800 Valley Road, Suite 110
Trussville, AL 35173
205-655-5260
www.sherrysfloralandcatering.com

Out of her desire to introduce down-home country cooking to a generation consumed by fast food, Sherry Merrifield established Sherry's Café in 2004 serving lunches consisting of delicious meats, piping hot vegetables, and homemade desserts. Sherry's southern fried chicken, pot roast, and mac & cheese receive rave reviews from customers who say "to die for," "best ever," and more! A local favorite are the homemade desserts—hot fudge cake, lemon pie, or peanut butter pie will make your mouth water and send your senses into overdrive. With 35 years experience, Sherry's continues to offer complete catering services with all the bells and whistles for office parties, rehearsal dinners, and weddings including beautifully decorated cakes and fresh flowers.

LUNCH
Monday – Saturday:
11:00 am to 2:00 pm
Sunday: 10:30 am to 2:30 pm
DINNER
Monday – Friday: 4:30 pm to 7:30 pm

Strawberry Cake

1 box white cake mix

4 eggs, beaten

1 cup frozen sliced strawberries with sugar, thawed

1 cup vegetable oil

1 (3-ounce) box strawberry Jell-O

½ cup milk

Using an electric mixer, combine cake ingredients until well mixed and batter is free of lumps. Grease and flour 2 (9-inch) round cake pans. Divide batter equally between the 2 pans. Bake at 350° about 30 minutes or until done. Cool in pans before removing.

Cream Cheese Frosting:

1 (8-ounce) package cream cheese, softened

1 stick butter, softened

1½ (16-ounce) boxes powdered sugar

1 teaspoon vanilla extract

½ teaspoon salt

Toasted chopped pecans, optional

Using electric mixer, combine cream cheese and butter. Add powdered sugar slowly until all sugar is used. Add vanilla and salt; mix well. Spread between layers and on sides and top of cake. Sprinkle with toasted chopped pecans, if desired.

Restaurant Recipe

Chicken Casserole

6 boneless chicken breasts

1 teaspoon salt

2 (10.75-ounce) cans cream of mushroom soup

1 (16-ounce) carton sour cream

1½ teaspoons onion powder

1 teaspoon pepper

2 sleeves Ritz crackers, crushed

½ cup butter, melted

Cover chicken with water; add salt. Boil over medium heat until chicken reaches 165°. Remove from water and cool. When cool, chop into bite-size pieces. Combine soup, sour cream, onion powder and pepper to make a sauce. Stir in chopped chicken and pour into a 9x13-inch baking dish. Bake at 350° until bubbly. Combine crushed crackers and melted butter; mix well. Spread over top of casserole. Return to oven and bake an additional 10 minutes.

Restaurant Recipe

Chicken Stop Broccoli Salad

1 head broccoli
5 to 6 strips bacon, fried and crumbled
5 green onions, thinly sliced
½ cup raisins
1 cup mayonnaise
2 tablespoons vinegar
¼ cup sugar

Divide broccoli into florets and remove stems. Slice stems and place florets and sliced stems in a bowl. Stir in bacon, onions and raisins. In a separate bowl, stir together mayonnaise, vinegar and sugar. Pour over broccoli mixture and stir well. Refrigerate until ready to serve. This recipe is best when made the night before or at least several hours before served.

Family Favorite

Chicken Stop

2824 Phillips Road Southwest
Lanett, AL 36863
334-576-2020

The Chicken Stop, opened in 1993, specializes in fried and grilled chicken fingers. They are also known as "The Place" for the best fried catfish in the area. For a nice change of pace, try their specialty salads and sandwiches. Meals are served with a choice of delicious sides prepared in-house. To finish, there are a variety of homemade cakes and pies available. So, when you are in town, don't forget to STOP at the Chicken Stop.

Monday – Wednesday:
10:30 am to 8:30 pm
Thursday – Saturday:
10:30 am to 9:00 pm

Best Catfish in Town

Real Open Pit BBQ

Potato Soup

1 cup chopped onion

32 ounces hash browns

3 cups water

14 ounces chicken broth

2 cups cream

1 (10.75-ounce) can cream of chicken soup

1 (10.75-ounce) can cream of celery soup

Salt and pepper to taste

Shredded cheese to taste

Crumbled bacon to taste

Boil onion and hash browns in water and broth for 30 minutes (do not overcook). Add cream, soups and salt and pepper. Serve with shredded cheese and crumbled bacon

Family Favorite

Roasted Sweet Potatoes

3 sweet potatoes, peeled

2 tablespoons butter, melted

2 tablespoons brown sugar

1 teaspoon ground cinnamon

¼ teaspoon ground nutmeg, optional

Pinch ground ginger, optional

Sea salt

Preheat oven to 350°. Coat a 2-quart glass baking dish with nonstick cooking spray. Dice peeled sweet potatoes into bite-size cubes; spread evenly in baking dish. Pour melted butter over top then sprinkle on brown sugar, cinnamon, nutmeg and ginger. Season with salt to taste. Mix gently to complete coat potatoes. Bake 60 minutes, stirring once or twice during roasting time.

Local Favorite

Milano's Grille

373 Fob James Drive
Valley, AL 36854
334-756-0605
www.milanosgrille.com

Since 1976, John Couscos, a Greek immigrant, has been serving top quality food in the restaurants he owned and operated throughout Tennessee and Georgia. John and his wife, Pam, finally landed in Valley, Alabama, and opened Milano's Grille. Utilizing traditional Greek and Italian recipes, they have created a truly authentic dining experience. From their Grecian shish kebab to homemade lasagna, Chicken Marsala to the Souvlaki Wrap, there is delicious food to please every diner. Milano's takes pride in making every customer feel like they are part of the family, so we know you will love it, too.

Monday – Saturday:
11:00 am to 10:30 pm
Sunday: Noon to 10:30 pm

DESOTO CAVERNS
Childersburg, Alabama

DeSoto Caverns is the first recorded cave in the United States and is well-known for having one of the largest continuing accumulations of onyx-marble stalagmites and stalactites in the world. There are many local legends about the cave, including that it was inhabited by Native Americans, it was a source of minerals used in the Civil War, and that during WWII there was a dance floor and honky-tonk in the huge main room. Visitors can tour the caverns beginning in that main underground room which is 12 stories high and larger than a football field. On the tour you will see thousands of cave formations—one of the most concentrated collections in America. Every tour features a light show inside the caverns—the most popular is the Creation Light Show based on the book of Genesis.

For more information on DeSoto Caverns and the DeSoto Caverns Family Fun Park, visit www.desotocavernspark.com

Big Daddy's BBQ

407 Main Street North
Warrior, AL 35180
205-590-2279

Big Daddy's BBQ, established October 2006, is a family-owned and operated restaurant serving nothing but the highest quality products. At Big Daddy's they cook just like they're cooking for family because everyone that visits is considered family. Try their award-winning ribs, pork, and chicken and some of the best catfish around. A local favorite is their signature sides including homemade macaroni & cheese, turnip greens, collard greens, and Big Daddy's famous fried corn on the cob. Don't leave without trying one of their homemade desserts—key lime cake, banana pudding, heavenly pie and peanut butter pie are some of the favorites.

Tuesday & Wednesday:
11:00 am to 3:00 pm
Thursday: 11:00 am to 7:00 pm
Friday: 11:00 am to 9:00 pm
Saturday: 11:00 am to 8:00 pm

Macaroni & Cheese

1 (16-ounce) package elbow macaroni

¼ teaspoon seasoned salt

⅛ teaspoon freshly ground black pepper

1 stick butter, melted

2 large eggs, lightly beaten

1 (8-ounce) package Velveeta, cut into small cubes

½ cup shredded mild Cheddar cheese, plus extra for top

½ cup shredded sharp Cheddar cheese, plus extra for top

1 tablespoon vegetable oil

2 cups evaporated milk

Boil noodles until tender, approximately 7 minutes over medium-high heat. Drain noodles; rinse in cool water. Add noodles to a large mixing bowl, stir in salt and pepper. Add melted butter; mix. Add beaten eggs and mix well. Add all three cheeses. Stir in vegetable oil and evaporated milk. Pour into a 9x13-inch baking dish. Sprinkle top with additional cheese. Bake at 350° for 45 minutes or until cheese is golden brown. Serve hot your favorite meats and veggies.

Restaurant Recipe

Pecan Cheese Log

1 (8-ounce) package cream cheese, softened

1 cup crumbled blue cheese

1 cup grated Swiss cheese

½ teaspoon hot sauce

¼ cup chopped pecans

In a medium bowl, combine all 3 cheeses and hot sauce, being sure they are mixed well. Shape into an 8-inch-long log (if you have time to refrigerate it for an hour in the bowl, it is easier to shape into a log when chilled). Wrap in plastic wrap, and chill 1 hour or longer. Roll in chopped pecans, and chill until ready to serve. Serve with crackers.

Local Favorite

White House Restaurant

9830 Highway 31
Warrior, AL 35180
205-647-2448

Good food, good times and good people... White House Restaurant is a family-owned, family-operated, and family-oriented business that believes the customer always comes first. The buffet features home-cooked favorites or you can order off the menu. Weekends feature steak and catfish. The service is friendly and the food tastes great at an affordable price. When you go, be sure to get a piece of their amazing peach cobbler which is made fresh daily and is the best you will get anywhere.

Sunday:
10:30 am to 4:00 pm
Monday – Saturday:
10:30 am to 8:00 pm

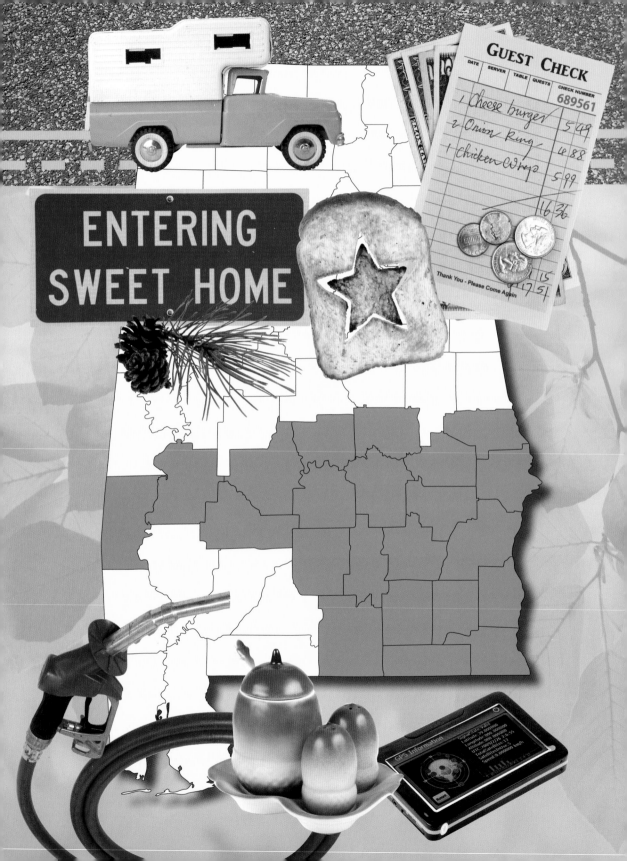

River REGION

Huggin' Molly's

129 Kirkland Street
Abbeville, AL 36310
334-585-7000
www.hugginmollys.com

An old-fashioned soda fountain and fine-dining restaurant, Huggin' Molly's lives up to the claim of being "frozen in the fifties." Decorated with one-of-a-kind antiques, the interior harkens back to another time—when drugstores had soda fountains with swivel stools and glass decanters full of brightly colored candies. Huggin' Molly's uses the tastiest ingredients to prepare widely varied lunch and dinner menus. The lunch menu features delicious sandwiches and homemade entrées featuring recipes from the 1950s. Nighttime dining features delicious appetizers, soups, salads, and over twenty entrées. And, of course, there are tasty treats from the old-fashioned soda fountain including sundaes, floats, milkshakes, and desserts.

Monday – Wednesday:
11:00 am to 2:00 pm
Thursday – Saturday:
11:00 am to 9:00 pm
Sunday Brunch: 11:00 am to 2:00 pm

Maryland–Style Crab Cakes

1 yellow bell pepper, chopped
1 green bell pepper, chopped
1 red bell pepper, chopped
1 red onion, chopped
3 tablespoons butter
1 pound lump crabmeat
4 tablespoons Old Bay seasoning
½ cup mayonnaise
2 eggs, beaten
2 cups panko breadcrumbs

Sauté peppers and onion in butter; remove from heat. Once cooled, transfer to mixing bowl and add crabmeat, Old Bay seasoning, mayonnaise, eggs and breadcrumbs. Mix well. Form into round "cakes." Use just enough vegetable oil to coat a frying pan and pan-fry on medium heat until golden brown on each side. Delicious served with fresh lemon and rémoulade sauce.

Restaurant Recipe

THE CITY OF DOGWOODS
Abbeville, Alabama

The Indian name for Abbie Creek was Yatta Abba which means "a grove of dogwood trees." Today, Abbeville is "The City of Dogwoods," and dogwoods still bloom along the creek and in the city. How do we know Abbeville is the #1 city? It's the first city, alphabetically, both by city and state, in the Rand McNally Road Atlas.

Amsterdam Café

410 South Gay Street
Auburn, AL 36830
334-826-8181
www.amsterdamcafeauburn.com

Amsterdam Café welcomes the opportunity to share their family's interpretation of the "Auburn Experience" with you and your family. The restaurant has been instrumental in re-establishing the "fresh from farm to table" principle which they consider to be vital to the community. The bounty of artisanal and house-made ingredients, exceptionally fresh seafood, and exquisite offerings of local farm-fresh produce are all highlighted within a unique menu. You are invited to enjoy "today" at Amsterdam Café while they forge a future for local Auburn dining that re-defines and re-invents the principles of southern hospitality.

Sunday – Thursday: 11:00 am to 9:00 pm • Friday & Saturday: 11:00 am to 10:00 pm

Crab Cake & Avocado Sandwich

Lump crab cake, avocado, Creole rémoulade, mango pico de gallo, toasted croissant—this sandwich has been featured as a top 100 dish of Alabama for the past eight years and has been a favorite among our customers since it was first put onto our menu.

Crab Cake:

1 (1-pound) can lump crabmeat

2 eggs, beaten

2 green onions, chopped

Juice of ½ lemon

1 teaspoon salt

¾ teaspoon pepper

1 teaspoon oregano

1 teaspoon thyme

3 teaspoons Old Bay seasoning

1 tablespoon Crystal hot sauce

¾ cup mayonnaise

4 cups panko breadcrumbs

1 avocado, sliced

Combine ingredients, except avocado, in a large mixing bowl and mix by hand. Portion mixture into desired size for each crab cake. Heat 1 tablespoon vegetable oil in a large skillet. Cook crab cakes thoroughly on both sides. Serve on a toasted croissant with fresh sliced avocado, house-made Mango Pico de Gallo and Creole Rémoulade.

Mango Pico de Gallo:

1 cup finely diced mango

3 tomatoes, diced

½ onion, diced

2½ jalapeños, diced

½ bunch cilantro, chopped

Salt and pepper to taste

Hot sauce to taste

Combine all ingredients and mix by hand.

Creole Rémoulade:

2 cups mayonnaise

½ cup Creole mustard

1 clove garlic, grated

Juice of ½ lemon

2 teaspoons minced shallots

2 teaspoons chopped dill

2 teaspoons chopped capers

2 teaspoons chopped basil

1½ tablespoons chopped green onion

¼ teaspoon paprika

Salt and pepper to taste

Combine all ingredients and mix by hand.

Restaurant Recipe

Pannie-George's Kitchen

2328 South College Street, Suite 6
Auburn, AL 36832
334-821-4142
www.panniegeorgeskitchen.com

The name Pannie-George's honors the owner's grandparents, Mary "Pannie" and George Taylor, to pay respect for their impact on the lives of their children and community. Cooking for large family gatherings equipped Pannie and George's children with ample knowledge of how to cook great southern-style food to please a crowd. The restaurant offers southern-style meat and vegetables that vary each day to provide an array of choices. Pannie-George's is not just a restaurant where people come and eat, it is the place where everyone is welcomed and treated like a respected member of the family. As they say, "The main ingredient in our food is LOVE."

Sunday: 10:30 am to 3:00 pm
Monday –Tuesday: 11:00 am to 2:00 pm
Wednesday – Friday: 11:00 am to 7:00 pm

Broccoli Cornbread

1 cup plain cornmeal

⅓ cup all-purpose flour

¾ teaspoon salt

1½ teaspoons baking powder

¼ teaspoon baking soda

5 eggs, slightly beaten

1 (10-ounce) package frozen chopped broccoli, thawed and drained

1 medium onion, chopped

2 cups shredded Cheddar cheese

1 (12-ounce) carton small curd cottage cheese

¾ cup butter, melted

Preheat oven to 350° and heat muffin pans for 10 minutes. In the meantime, in a bowl combine cornmeal, flour, salt, baking powder and baking soda. In another bowl, combine the eggs, broccoli, onion, cheeses and butter. Add cornmeal mixture to the egg mixture and stir until just moistened, don't over mix. Remove muffin pans from oven with an oven mitt and spray each well with nonstick cooking spray. Fill each well with ¼ cup of batter. Bake at 350° for about 35 minutes.

Family Favorite

Smothered Pork Chops with Mushrooms

3 tablespoons vegetable oil, divided

2 tablespoons butter, divided

4 (8-ounce) center cut pork chops

½ teaspoon seasoned salt,
plus more to taste

¼ teaspoon coarse ground
black pepper

1 medium onion, chopped

2 celery ribs, chopped

½ medium red bell pepper, seeded and
chopped (about ½ cup)

2 garlic cloves, chopped

10 ounces fresh mushrooms, sliced
(your choice)

3 tablespoons all-purpose flour

1½ teaspoons chopped fresh thyme
or ½ teaspoon dried

1 cup chicken broth or water

1 cup milk

In a large skillet, heat 2 tablespoons oil and 1 tablespoon butter over medium-low heat. Season the pork chops with seasoned salt and pepper on both sides. Cook until browned, about 2 minutes on each side. Transfer to a plate and set aside.

Reduce heat to medium and add remaining 1 tablespoon oil and 1 tablespoon butter to the skillet. Add the onion, celery, red bell pepper and garlic. Cook stirring often, until softened, about 3 minutes. Add mushrooms and cook until they give off their liquid, it evaporates and they begin to brown, about 8 minutes.

Sprinkle the vegetables with the flour and thyme and stir well. Stir in the broth and milk and bring to a simmer. Return the pork chops and any juice on the plate to the skillet and cover. Cook stirring occasionally, until the pork chops show no sign of pink when pierced at the bone, 25 to 30 minutes. Serve with rice or mashed potatoes.

Makes 4 servings.

Family Favorite

THINKSTOCK/ISTOCK/ROMANKORYTOV

Mulligan Stew

1 small yellow onion, finely chopped

½ stalk celery, finely chopped

2 tablespoons vegetable oil

1 pound ground chuck

1 tablespoon seasoned salt

½ teaspoon garlic salt

1½ teaspoons chili powder

2 tablespoons yellow mustard

1 tablespoon Worcestershire sauce

2 (8-ounce) cans tomato sauce

½ cup ketchup

24 ounces water

1 (12-ounce) package elbow macaroni

In a large pot, cook onion and celery in oil until translucent. Add meat and cook until almost brown. Add spices, mustard and Worcestershire; stir well and cook 5 minutes to allow spices to heat through meat. Add tomato sauce, ketchup and water; simmer 30 minutes. Add macaroni; stir. When macaroni is done, serve and enjoy.

Local Favorite

Strawberry Cucumber Salad

1 pint strawberries

2 large cucumbers

1 cup mayonnaise

⅛ cup sugar

2 tablespoons pepper, or to taste

Wash strawberries well, remove tops and slice (should have about 3 cups). Peel cucumbers and chop (should have about 3 cups). Combine mayonnaise and sugar; stir until sugar is fully dissolved. Add pepper.

Local Favorite

Hamburger Steak

12 ounces lean ground beef

Salt and pepper

½ medium onion, sliced

1 tablespoon vegetable oil

2 tablespoons all-purpose flour

1 cup beef broth

Season beef with salt and pepper to taste. Pat it out and form into the shape of a steak. Grill about 4½ minutes on each side or until fully cooked. Grill onions to golden brown. Heat oil in a skillet; stir in flour with a fork. Season to taste with salt and pepper and mix well. Slowly add broth while constantly stirring. Simmer, stirring occasionally, 5 minutes or until gravy thickens. Plate meat, top with onions then gravy. Makes 1 serving.

Restaurant Recipe

Winter's Restaurant

40 Camden Bypass
Camden, AL 36726
334-682-5010

Built around 1981 and located in a brick building with white columns, Winter's Restaurant is a full-service restaurant and bar. Located in the neat Southern Inn Motel and across from McGraw-Webb Chevrolet, there is plenty of parking space and a wheelchair ramp. Inside you will see area wildlife mounted and placed on the walls. Visit for the best food you will ever eat.

Monday – Saturday: 6:00 am to 9:00 pm

The Castle Café

1 Sansbury Street
Daleville, AL 36322
334-598-9005

The Castle Café, established in 1989, brings together a unique blend of old-world Germany and today's southern hospitality. Having immigrated shortly after WWII from Buchen, Germany, a small town situated in the Odenwald low mountain range, the restaurant's matriarch, Ingrid Strange, brought with her many of her family's traditional German recipes. Miss Ingrid prides herself on authentic German-style preparation and presentation for the cuisine. From handmade Jaeger Schnitzel to European-style cheesecakes, the dining experience is like no other in the Wiregrass, the state of Alabama, or the southeast United States.

Monday – Friday: 9:30 am to 2:30 pm
Saturday: 9:30 am to 1:00 pm

German Potato Salad

6 to 8 red potatoes
½ pound bacon
1 onion, minced
½ to ¾ cup vinegar
½ to ¾ cup beef stock
2 tablespoons minced parsley
Salt to taste
1 teaspoon white pepper

Place unpeeled potatoes in a large stockpot and cover completely with water; salt lightly. Cover pot and bring to a boil. Reduce heat to medium and cook until potatoes are done yet firm. (Do not overcook potatoes or they will fall apart in the salad.) Peel potatoes while they are still hot and cut into thin slices. Fry bacon in a saucepan; when golden, but not yet brown or crisp, add onions. Sauté slowly until onions become transparent but not golden. Remove from heat. Combine vinegar and beef stock; add to stockpot pouring carefully so the liquid does not cause the hot bacon fat to splatter. Return pot to medium-high heat and bring to boil; pour over sliced potatoes. Using a wooden spatula, gently lift potatoes slightly so dressing runs over them evenly. Sprinkle with parsley and season with salt and pepper.

Restaurant Recipe

Sweet Potato Casserole

3 cups mashed sweet potatoes

¾ cup plus 1 tablespoon sugar

½ cup plus 3 tablespoons margarine, softened

1 teaspoon vanilla extract

2 eggs, beaten

2 to 3 cups miniature marshmallows

Combine sweet potatoes, sugar, margarine and vanilla in bowl and mix well. Add eggs; mix well again making sure eggs are incorporated. Pour into buttered 2-quart casserole dish. Cover top completely with miniature marshmallows and bake at 350° for 30 minutes. Marshmallows should be light golden brown. Enjoy.

Restaurant Recipe

Blue Plate Restaurant

3850 West Main Street
Dothan, AL 36305
334-702-7100
www.blueplaterestaurant.com

Not your average dining experience, the Blue Plate Restaurant features a menu with a variety wide enough to satisfy any sized appetite, all tastefully prepared in the true southern tradition. The warm and inviting décor evokes a modern, laid-back atmosphere that is both sophisticated and casual. Servers are prompt and food is plentiful. It is nice to know that with today's fast-paced and busy lifestyle, there is a place where families can gather around the table, catch up with each other and with friends while enjoying great southern cooking. The Blue Plate is sure to provide a memorable dining experience.

Monday – Friday: 10:30 am to 8:30 pm
Sunday: 10:30 am to 3:00 pm

The Old Mill Restaurant

2557 Murphy Mill Road
Dothan, AL 36303
334-794-8530
www.oldmilldothan.com

The Old Mill Restaurant opened December 1986. Partners Bill Slavins and Bob Watson combined their years of restaurant expertise to bring to Dothan a new dining experience. Their full-service, full-menu restaurant offers top-quality steaks char-grilled with a special sauce and fresh char-grilled Gulf of Mexico seafood. Signature items include certified Angus beef rib-eye and filet mignon and fresh Gulf grouper. The Old Mill grouper fingers are designated one of the "100 Dishes to Eat in Alabama Before You Die" by yearofalabamafood.com. This is a great place for casual dinner or to celebrate special events in one of three private rooms.

LUNCH
Monday – Friday: 11:00 am to 2:00 pm
DINNER
Monday – Saturday: 4:30 pm to 9:00 pm

Peanut Butter Pies

12 cups (1½ gallons) vanilla ice cream, softened
24 ounces crunchy peanut butter
1 (16-ounce) carton Cool Whip
4 (8-inch) Oreo cookie crumb pie crusts, frozen

Mix all ingredients in a large mixing bowl. Pour into frozen Oreo cookie crumb crusts and refreeze. Thaw about 10 minutes before serving. Makes 4 pies.

Restaurant Recipe

Grecian Grouper

8 ounces fresh Gulf grouper
2 tablespoons (1 ounce) virgin olive oil
¼ cup (2 ounces) grated Parmesan cheese
1 teaspoon freshly chopped green onion

Brush grouper with half of the olive oil. Char-grill until done. Coat grouper with remaining olive oil, sprinkle Parmesan cheese on top and put in broiler until cheese is toasted. Top with green onions and serve.

Restaurant Recipe

PEANUT CAPITAL OF THE WORLD
Dothan, Alabama

This place is NUTS. With about a fourth of the US peanut crop produced within 75 miles of Dothan, and much of it processed in the city, Dothan is called The Peanut Capital of the World. A large, gold peanut welcomes you to the Visitors Center. Five-foot-tall peanut sculptures, each individually decorated, can be found around Dothan—including an Elvis-themed peanut inside the Visitors Center. If that's not nutty enough, come back in November for the National Peanut Festival.

For more information: www.dothan.org

Zack's Family Restaurant

1495 Headland Avenue
Dothan, AL 36303
334-673-9225

Zack's Family Restaurant was started in 1995 featuring Zack's favorite family recipes including steak, shrimp, and a variety of "southern-style" favorites. In 1997, Zack opened the Slocomb location where Zack's recipes continued to be developed and become perfected. It was after opening the Slocomb location that Zack's restaurant concept of "good old-fashioned southern cooking" was defined. Zack has expanded to two additional locations in Dothan and Enterprise. Zack's rule for the customer is to act as if you are at grandma's home and enjoy yourself. Join them and enjoy a great southern meal!

Sunday – Friday: 10:30 am to 2:30 pm

Broccoli Casserole

4 (8-ounce) packages frozen chopped broccoli

2 (10-ounce) cans cream of mushroom soup

1½ cups mayonnaise

3 cups shredded cheese

3 eggs, beaten

1 (4-ounce) jar diced pimento

1 onion, finely chopped

1 (6-ounce) jar sliced mushrooms

Salt and pepper to taste

3 cups Ritz crackers, crushed

3 tablespoons butter, melted

Cook broccoli per package directions; drain. Combine soup, mayonnaise, cheese, eggs, pimento, onion and mushrooms; add to broccoli. Season with salt and pepper. Pour into greased 9x13-inch casserole dish. Mix crackers and butter; sprinkle over casserole. Bake at 350° for 30 minutes.

Restaurant Recipe

Fried Green Tomatoes

8 cups water

1 egg, beaten

2 tablespoons honey Dijon mustard

Sliced green tomatoes

Zack's Breader

Salt and pepper to taste

Create an egg wash by combining water, egg and mustard. Dip each tomato slice in egg wash, then roll in Zack's Breader. Dip again in egg wash and then back in Zack's Breader. Deep fry at 350° for 4 minutes.

Restaurant Recipe

*Zack's Breader is available at Zack's Family Restaurant or may be substituted with seasoned cornmeal.

Key Lime Cake

Cake:

1 box lemon supreme cake mix

4 eggs, beaten

1 (3-ounce) package lime Jell-O

¾ cup orange juice

1⅓ cups cooking oil

Combine all ingredients. Pour into 3 greased and floured 9-inch cake pans. Bake according to box instructions. Allow to cool.

Lime Frosting:

1 (8-ounce) package cream cheese, softened

½ cup butter, softened

1 (16-ounce) box powdered sugar

3 tablespoons fresh lime (or lemon) juice

In a large bowl, beat cream cheese and butter until light and fluffy. Add powdered sugar and juice; mix well. Spread onto cooled cake.

Restaurant Recipe

Amazing Grace Café

18320 Andalusia Highway
Dozier, AL 36028
334-496-2525

Amazing Grace Café is about heritage for owner Patricia Grace. Her love of serving delicious food was fostered as a child growing up in the mid-1950's on her grandmother's 60-acre farm in rural Alabama. When friends, neighbors, and family helped attend crops, her grandmother's sisters would serve dinner fresh from the garden and smokehouse. Seeing everyone enjoying each other and the meal convinced Patricia this was a scene she wanted to see played over and over. And this is exactly what happens in her restaurant where delicious fresh food is served to honor that old style and tradition of cooking.

Tuesday – Saturday:
6:00 am to 3:00 pm
Sunday:
11:00 am to 3:00 pm

Fried Ribs

Yep, that's what I said, Fried Ribs. In the South, we will fry anything we can catch.

Oil for frying

8 to 10 riblets strips (or feather bones is another name)

3 eggs, beaten

½ cup buttermilk

4 cups self-rising flour

Garlic powder, black pepper and seasoned salt to taste

Heat at least 2 inches oil in a heavy iron pot (preferable) or frying pan to 300°. Wash meat with cool water; pat dry and place in a bowl. Blend eggs and buttermilk. Pour over ribs and stir to coat well. Mix flour and seasonings, then dredge strips through flour until all sides are covered (work in batches only flouring the amount you are frying). Gently place meat in oil and brown to your desired color, turning only once. Now that's good eating. Serves 3 to 4 people.

Restaurant Recipe

Glazed Club Quesadillas

Glaze:

½ cup balsamic vinegar

½ teaspoon melted butter

5 heaping tablespoons sugar

Combine glaze ingredients in a small saucepan over medium-high heat. Whisk until boiling. Set aside to cool while preparing quesadillas.

Quesadillas:

8 chicken strips

4 extra-large flour tortillas

1 cup shredded mozzarella cheese

8 strips bacon, cooked crispy

Pan-sear chicken strips for 5 to 8 minutes or until done. Working in batches, butter one side of a tortilla and place butter side down in a skillet over medium heat. Sprinkle cheese on top of tortilla. When cheese is beginning to melt, dice 2 chicken strips and spread evenly over cheese. Dice two slices bacon and spread over chicken. When cheese is completely melted, fold tortilla over. If needed, continue to cook until outside shell is golden brown. Brush with glaze while hot. Serve. Repeat 3 more times to make 4 servings.

Restaurant Recipe

Annie's Café

212 North Main Street
Enterprise, AL 36330
334-347-6622

What started years ago as a local pool hall and burger joint has been transformed into the town's best café by owners Jeffery and Matthew Larson. Fresh, never frozen, hand-pattied burgers, made by "Momma," are voted #1 in the Wiregrass three years and running. The menu doesn't stop there. Hand-cut, Sterling Silver, prime-choice rib-eyes and filets are a must-eat, and were nominated for "Best Steak in Alabama." From chicken salad to bulgogi, the menu is large and diverse with dishes all made from scratch. At Annie's Café you are guaranteed food that is served fresh, homemade, and cooked to order.

Monday – Friday: 6:00 am to 8:30 pm

Cutts Restaurant

417 East Lee Street
Enterprise, AL 36330
334-347-1110

In 1967, a small country store in south Alabama became famous for their chili dog. Then in 1974, this small country store relocated to Enterprise and became Cutts Snack Bar. Rick and Liane Cutts, the current owners, grew Cutts Snack Bar into Cutts Restaurant in 1992, and that is where it has been ever since. Dining at Cutts Restaurant transports you to the days of good ole' country cooking, reminding us that quality food and good service are what's most important. Named in "100 Dishes to Eat in Alabama Before You Die," Cutts serves breakfast, lunch, and dinner. They even still serve that famous chili dog and are a landmark in Enterprise. A family atmosphere and cookin' like your mamma and grandmamma made it is what they do best. As they like to say, Cutts Restaurant, "a family restaurant, yours and ours."

Monday – Friday: 8:00 am to 8:00 pm
Saturday:
10:00 am to 2:00 pm, short orders only

Sisters' Tater Tot Casserole

1 pound ground hamburger meat
1 (10.75-ounce) can cream of mushroom soup
1 green bell pepper, optional
1 (16-ounce) bag tater tots
Shredded cheese

Preheat your oven to 350°. Brown hamburger meat in a skillet; drain. Return to the skillet and add cream of mushroom soup. Stir continuously. Simmer in skillet on low heat for 10 minutes. Finely chop green bell pepper, if desired, and add to mixture. Place mixture in a 2-quart casserole dish and lay tater tots neatly on top. Bake until tater tots are brown (about 25 to 30 minutes). Sprinkle generously with cheese and return to oven just until cheese is melted. Serves 6.

Restaurant Recipe

Southern Bacon Macaroni and Cheese

1 (7-ounce) package elbow macaroni

3 tablespoons butter

3 tablespoons all-purpose flour

¼ teaspoon salt

Dash pepper

1 cup milk

1½ cups shredded Cheddar cheese

1 (12- to 16-ounce) package thick-sliced bacon, cooked crispy

Cook macaroni according to package directions. Meanwhile, in a large saucepan, melt butter over medium-low heat. Add flour, salt and pepper; stir until smooth. Gradually add milk. Bring to a boil; cook and stir until thickened (2 to 4 minutes). Remove from heat and stir in cheese until melted. Break bacon into bite-sized pieces. When pasta is done, drain well. Add cheese mixture and bacon; toss to coat. Enjoy! Serves 4.

Restaurant Recipe

Memaw's Apple Pie

Filling:

¾ cup sugar

2 tablespoons all-purpose flour

¾ teaspoon cinnamon

¼ teaspoon salt

⅛ teaspoon nutmeg

6 medium, thinly sliced, peeled apples

Crust:

1 recipe pastry for a 9-inch double-crust pie

Preheat oven to 425°. In a large bowl, combine filling ingredients, except apples. Mix well. Add apples and toss gently to mix. Line floured pie pan with pie crust; fill with the mixture. Top with second crust, seal edges and flute. Cut slits to vent. Bake 40 to 45 minutes or until apples are tender and crust is golden brown.

Restaurant Recipe

Homemade pies are a favorite with loyal customers. Misty and Lindsey Cotts proudly display the daily specialties.

Southern Broadway Dinner Theater

104 North Main Street
Enterprise, AL 36330
334-470-6568
www.southernbroadway.com

Southern Broadway Dinner Theater is a jewel in south Alabama's Wiregrass region. The dinner theater productions are held throughout the year in the beautiful historic downtown Enterprise in a unique venue with special charm. The menus are superb; every meal a perfect accompaniment to the production and outstandingly presented in a family-friendly style while dinner music from the era of the show's setting captures the mood for the show. The original shows range from historical dramas to up-beat musicals with everything in between, and features fine talent from the local area and beyond. Dinner and a show with Southern Broadway is definitely an evening worth experiencing!

Call or visit online for show schedules.

Skillet Apple Pie

3 Granny Smith apples
3 Gala apples
1 teaspoon ground cinnamon
¾ cup plus 2 tablespoons sugar, divided
1 stick butter
1 cup firmly packed brown sugar
1 (2-crust) package refrigerated pie crusts
1 egg white

Preheat oven to 350°. Peel apples and cut into wedges. Toss cut apples with cinnamon and ¾ cup sugar in a gallon-sized zip-close bag. Melt butter in a 10-inch iron skillet; remove from heat and add brown sugar. Stir until smooth and velvety. Unroll 1 pie crust. Place on top of brown sugar mixture in the skillet. Pour apple mixture over pie crust. Place second pie crust on top. Whisk egg white until foamy. Brush top of pie crust with egg white and sprinkle with 2 tablespoons sugar. Cut 4 to 5 slits in top middle section of pie crust. Bake 1 hour or until golden brown and bubbly. Cool 30 minutes before serving.

Restaurant Recipe

BOLL WEEVIL MONUMENT
December 11, 1919

In profound appreciation of the Boll Weevil and what it has done as the Herald of Prosperity this monument was erected by the Citizens of Enterprise, Coffee County, Alabama

ALABAMA HISTORICAL ASSOCIATION 1974

BOLL WEEVIL MONUMENT

Enterprise, Alabama

The world's only boll weevil monument is located in the middle of Main Street in Enterprise. The large monument depicts a woman holding a boll weevil aloft. Why a boll weevil? In 1915, an infestation of boll weevils destroyed most of the cotton crops in Coffee County. Facing economic ruin, the area farmers were forced to diversify, planting peanuts and other crops in an effort to lessen the damage. Within two years, Coffee County was the leading producer of peanuts in the US. In appreciation, a monument was erected in the city center as a reminder of how the city's residents adjusted in the face of adversity.

For more information,
visit www.cityofenterprise.net.

The Cajun Corner

**114 North Eufaula Avenue, Suite 4
Eufaula, AL 36027
334-616-0816
www.thecajuncorner.com**

Cajun Corner, the place to eat in Eufaula, is where you can let the good times roll or "Laissez les bons temps rouler" as they say down in Nawlins. Put some South in your mouth with hand-breaded, deep-fried eggplant sticks served with homemade rémoulade dipping sauce. The signature New Orleans Stuffed Fish is a local favorite. Taste the Creole flavor of Mardis Gras Stuffed Shrimp or North Shore Pasta. You'll enjoy it all from cocktails, appetizers, amazing salads, steaks, seafood, and pasta to tempting desserts you can't resist. Y'all have a ball at Cajun Corner and they'll serve you like the Kings and Queens of Mardis Gras!

**Sunday – Thursday: 11:00 am to 9:00 pm
Friday – Saturday: 11:00 am to 10:00 pm**

Stewed Chicken & Andouille

2½ pounds cleaned chicken breast meat, cut into strips

1 tablespoon Cajun spice

½ cup flour, divided

¼ cup vegetable oil

1 pound andouille sausage, cut into ½-inch slices

2 cups chopped onion

1 cup chopped celery

½ cup chopped bell pepper

4 bay leaves

2 tablespoons minced garlic

6 cups chicken stock

½ teaspoon salt

½ teaspoon cayenne

¼ cup chopped parsley

¼ cup chopped green onion

Season chicken with Cajun spice and coat with ¼ cup flour. Heat oil in large Dutch oven, brown chicken. Add andouille and remaining ¼ cup flour; mix well. Cook 2 to 3 minutes. Add onion, celery and bell pepper; mix well and cook 5 to 6 minutes. Add bay leaves and garlic; mix well. Add stock, salt and cayenne. Bring to a boil then reduce heat to medium low. Cook uncovered for 1 hour. Remove bay leaves. Add parsley and green onion and serve immediately.

Restaurant Recipe

Bacon Jalapeño Poppers

1 (8-ounce) package cream cheese,
softened

¼ cup shredded sharp Cheddar cheese

¼ cup chopped green onions

2 tablespoons bacon bits

1 teaspoon lime juice

1 garlic clove, minced

Salt to taste

14 jalapeño peppers,
halved lengthwise and seeded

Hot sauce, optional

Preheat oven to 425°. Combine cream cheese, Cheddar cheese, green onions, bacon bits, lime juice, garlic and salt. Fill pepper halves with cheese mixture then place on baking sheet. Bake 15 to 20 minutes until hot and cheese is melted. Top with hot sauce, if desired. Serve immediately.

Restaurant Recipe

Phil's Barbecue

534 South Randolph Avenue
Eufaula, AL 36027
334-687-3337
www.bestbuttsinalabama.com

Phil's Barbecue, a family-owned restaurant in historic Eufaula, Alabama, has been in business since 1991. What makes them so successful? It is their goal to provide customers with the absolutely best quality products available which is accomplished by undying devotion from their management team and crew. Serving the "Best Butts in Alabama" plus many more options for delicious barbecue and sides, you are guaranteed to enjoy your visit to Phil's Barbecue, Winner of 2013 Alabama BBQ Sauce-Off plus numerous other awards.

Monday – Thursday: 10:00 am to 7:30 pm
Friday & Saturday: 10:00 am to 8:00 pm
Sunday: 11:00 am to 3:00 pm

THINKSTOCK/ISTOCK/

Priester's Pecans

80 Bishop Bottom Road
Fort Deposit, AL 36032
334-227-8355
www.priesters.com

Priester's Pecans features a sandwich and salad cold bar or enjoy a truly southern meal of delicious meats and vegetables at the hot bar. Visit the food area filled with unusual items including pickles, syrups, gourmet coffee, salad dressings, jams, jellies, and 16 unique flavors of ice cream. The gift shop features unique and wonderful gifts. The viewing area upstairs is where you can watch the making of their homemade candies—see chocolates being enrobed, divinity and fudge being dipped, and cakes, pies and brownies being baked. Priester's is a family-owned company specializing in delicious pecan desserts, candies, pies, cakes, and bulk pecans.

Retail Store: 7 days a week:
8:00 am to 6:00 pm
Cold Bar: 10:00 am to 3:00 pm
Hot Bar: 11:00 am to 2:00 pm
Order online anytime at
www.priester.scom

Pecan Cream Cheese Squares

1 package yellow cake mix

½ cup margarine, softened

3 eggs, divided

2 cups chopped pecans

1 (8-ounce) package cream cheese, softened

1 (16-ounce) box powdered sugar

1 teaspoon butternut extract (can use vanilla as a substitute)

Preheat oven to 350°. Combine cake mix, margarine and 1 egg until well mixed. Stir in pecans; batter will be thick. Press into a greased 9x13-inch baking pan. Beat cream cheese, remaining 2 eggs and sugar until smooth. Add flavoring and mix well. Pour over pecan mixture. Bake 45 to 50 minutes or until golden brown. Cool before cutting into squares. Store in refrigerator.

Local Favorite

Homemade Peach Ice Cream

6 fresh ripe peaches, blended

1 tablespoon vanilla extract

Pinch salt

2 cups sugar

2 (8-ounce) cans sweetened condensed milk

Milk

Combine peaches, vanilla, salt, sugar and condensed milk in the freezing container of an electric ice cream machine; mix well. Add milk to reach the container's fill line. Follow manufacturer's instructions to freeze ice cream. A delicious summer treat.

Restaurant Recipe

The Old Barn Restaurant

**2146 County Rd 2243
Goshen, AL 36035
334-484-3200
www.oldbarnrestaurant.com**

Housed inside a beautiful 100-year-old barn atop a hill, The Old Barn Restaurant serves a full menu with steak, seafood, quail, burgers, and more, for dinner Thursday through Saturday nights and country cooking on Sunday. The Sunday meals include fresh vegetables grown by the family. Family owned (since 2006) by Scottie and Amy Chandler, and Amy's parents, Johnny and Beverly Taylor, The Old Barn Restaurant is known for its desserts made from recipes passed down from generation to generation as well as the best steaks around. Their Rum Bread Pudding and delicious seafood are local favorites. You are guaranteed great service and superb food at The Old Barn, don't miss it.

**Thursday – Saturday: 5:00 pm to 9:00 pm
Sunday Lunch: 11:00 am to 2:00 pm**

Red's Little School House

20 Gardner Road
Grady, AL 36036
334-584-7955

After passing this old school house every day of her life, Debbie went to her father, Red, and told him the property was now for sale. Debbie and Red had been cooking at the state fairs for a while, and she wanted a place that they could call their own. They bought the property in 1984 and started a resale store serving barbecue and camp stew. Now, this unique restaurant serves the finest in true southern cooking. The vegetables are grown out back so they are fresh for picking and cooking. The Lemon Icebox Pie and Fried Cornbread are truly worth the drive.

Wednesday – Saturday: 11:00 am to 9:00 pm
Sunday: 11:00 am to 3:00 pm

THINKSTOCK/ISTOCK/FOTOGAL

Cold-Oven Pound Cake

2 sticks butter, softened
½ cup shortening
3 cups sugar
6 eggs
¾ teaspoon baking powder
3 cups plain flour
1 cup buttermilk
½ teaspoon almond extract
½ teaspoon vanilla extract
¼ teaspoon yellow food coloring

Do not preheat oven. Cream butter, shortening and sugar. Add eggs, 1 at a time, mixing well after each. Add baking powder to flour. Add flour mixture to creamed mixture alternately with buttermilk mixing well after each addition. Add almond and vanilla along with the food coloring; mix well. Pour mixture in a tube or Bundt pan. Place in cold oven then set to 350°; bake 1½ hours (if using a pan without a hole, bake at 300° for 2 to 2½ hours).

Restaurant Recipe

Mini Cheesecakes

12 vanilla wafers
2 (8-ounce) packages cream cheese, softened
½ cup sugar
1 teaspoon vanilla extract
2 eggs, beaten

Line muffin tins with foil liners. Place 1 wafer in bottom of each liner. Combine cream cheese, sugar and vanilla using an electric mixer on medium speed. Add eggs and mix again. Pour over wafers filling to ¾ full. Bake 25 minutes at 325°. Remove from pan and cool before serving. If desired, top with fresh fruit, pie filling or preserves.

Restaurant Recipe

Southern Tomato Gravy

This is such a southern dish, served over biscuits for breakfast, rice or mashed potatoes for supper. Also good over pasta and leftover gravy can be used in hamburger dishes. A great way to use up all those tomatoes from the garden.

2 cups peeled and chopped fresh tomatoes (can use a 14.5-ounce can of tomatoes)

½ teaspoon salt

¼ teaspoon pepper

1 teaspoon sugar

¼ teaspoon garlic powder

5 tablespoons bacon drippings

5 tablespoons all-purpose flour

1¼ cups water (some prefer to use milk instead of water)

Place cut tomatoes in bowl. Add salt, pepper, sugar and garlic powder; mix with a spoon. Heat bacon drippings in a skillet on stovetop over high heat. Add flour and make a roux (cook until thick and caramel-colored). Pour in tomatoes and water and cook until the consistency of gravy. Serve hot over biscuits.

Restaurant Recipe

It Don't Matter

**18700 Montgomery Highway
Highland Home, AL 36041
334-537-4849**

It Don't Matter has just rebuilt after a horrific fire and now it is bigger and better than ever. Drop by for a hot and delicious breakfast cooked to order. Lunch is a daily buffet featuring several meats— their freshly cooked fried chicken is a favorite—plus 4 to 15 vegetables. Steaks are hand-cut daily, and Saturday nights feature an impressive seafood buffet. Don't miss It Don't Matter—Bigger & Better Than Before.

**Monday – Thursday: 6:00 am to 8:00 pm
Friday & Saturday: 6:00 am to 9:00 pm
Sunday: 6:00 am to 3:30 pm**

Shrimp Étouffée

6 tablespoons butter, divided

4 tablespoons flour

1 cup diced onion

½ cup diced celery

½ cup diced bell pepper

4 cloves garlic

1 teaspoon chopped thyme

2 cups shrimp stock

1 cup diced tomatoes

1 tablespoon Creole seasoning

1 tablespoon Worcestershire sauce

1 pound shrimp, shelled and deveined

Hot sauce to taste

Salt and pepper to taste

2 tablespoons lemon juice (½ lemon)

½ cup sliced green onion

¼ cup chopped parsley

Melt 4 tablespoons butter in a large saucepan over medium heat stirring until it starts to brown. While continuously mixing, sprinkle in flour and simmer until it turns dark brown, about 10 to 20 minutes. Add onion and celery; mix well. And peppers and cook until tender, about 8 to 10 minutes. Add garlic and thyme; cook 5 minutes more. Whisk in stock. Add tomatoes, Creole seasoning and Worcestershire sauce and simmer 20 minutes. Add shrimp and cook until done, about 5 minutes.

Season with hot sauce, salt and pepper to taste. Remove from heat and mix in remaining 2 tablespoons butter, lemon juice, green onion and parsley. Serve over cooked rice. Serves 4.

Tip: If you do not have shrimp stock, simmer the shrimp shells in chicken stock or beer for 30 minutes.

Family Favorite

Ezell's Fish Camp

776 Ezell Road • Lavaca, AL 36904
205-654-2205
Find us on Facebook

Ezell's Fish Camp is one of the South's oldest and most recognized restaurants. The original location opened in 1937 in Lavaca and is on the state of Alabama's directory which lists Ezell's coleslaw and hushpuppies as two of Alabama's 100 Dishes to Eat Before you Die. Now with five locations in Alabama (plus two in Mississippi), Ezell's has expanded their tradition of serving great catfish plus delicious sides, excellent steaks, other seafood, and so much more. Every location offers a casual, comfortable setting with terrific, friendly service. EAT CATFISH AND BE SOMEBODY.

Thursday:
11:00 am to 9:00 pm

Friday & Saturday:
11:00 am to 10:00 pm

Sunday:
11:00 am to 9:00 pm

Slaw

2 large heads cabbage, chopped

2 cups Duke's mayonnaise

2 cups sweet salad cubes
(sweet pickle relish), drained

½ cup sugar

½ cup ground yellow onions

Use no salt or pepper when mixing the slaw, it makes the cabbage weep. Combine all ingredients using more or less mayonnaise to your preferred consistency. Slaw is always better second day after tastes marry. Will last a few days if refrigerated.

Restaurant Recipe

Black Bean Queso

2 (15-ounce) cans black beans, drained and rinsed

2 (8-ounce) packages cream cheese, cubed

1 (8-ounce) box Velveeta, cubed

1 cup chunky salsa

1 tablespoon Cajun seasoning

2 tablespoons chopped fresh cilantro, optional

Salt and pepper to taste

Combine all ingredients in a slow cooker set to medium heat; allow to cook about 15 minutes or until cheese is melted. Stir to combine all ingredients. Cover, reduce heat to low and cook about 2 hours. When ready to serve, stir well and increase heat to medium. Serve right from the slow cooker with tortilla chips for dipping.

Local Favorite

Wagon Wheel, Too

**2534 Highway 14
Millbrook AL 36054
334-285-1007**

Wagon Wheel, Too is a Dixie tradition serving eye-opening breakfasts and meat and three specials to locals and visitors. Come early for a hearty made-to-order breakfast and then later for a lunch special featuring home-cooked dishes just like Grandmother made or come later for dinner ordering from a menu of delicious dishes. Some local favorites include the pork chop special, collard greens and peach cobbler. You've heard, "Go where the locals go if you want great food." Wagon Wheel, Too is exactly that kind of restaurant. The locals keep coming back for the great flavor and friendly service—you will too.

**Monday –Thursday: 6:00 am to 3:00 pm
Friday: 6:00 am to 9:00 pm
Saturday – Sunday: 6:00 am to 3:00 pm**

Farmers Market Café

315 North McDonough Street
Montgomery, AL 36104
334-262-1970 or 334-262-9163
www.farmersmarketcafe.net

Family operated since 1959, Farmers Market Café offers authentic southern, country-style cooking at its best. What began as a small counter offering light breakfasts and lunches of sandwiches and camp stew has grown into a full-service restaurant. In the early 1980's, Phil and JoAnn Norton purchased the café from the Cecil Tucker family. With good country cooking, friendliness, and a family atmosphere, the Norton Farmers Market Café makes your tummy happy. Order from the lunch menu or choose your meal from the serving line, but definitely try the Southern Fried Chicken which was featured in "The Best of Montgomery" 2011.

Monday – Friday:
Breakfast: 5:30 am to 11:00 am
Lunch: 11:00 am to 2:00 pm

Collard Soup

1 pound ham steak, bite-size pieces

1 pound smoked sausage, bite-size pieces

1 onion, chopped

1 garlic clove, minced (more or less to taste)

8 cups chicken stock

3 cups new potatoes, bite-size pieces with skin

3 (14-ounce) cans great Northern beans

1 (16-ounce) bag collards or 1 bunch chopped fresh collards

Salt and pepper

Sauté ham, sausage, onion and garlic until lightly browned. Add chicken stock, potatoes, beans and collards; salt and pepper to taste. Simmer about 1 hour or until collards and potatoes are tender. Enjoy!

Restaurant Recipe

THINKSTOCK/ISTOCK/YULIA DAVIDOVICH

Cinnamon Apple Cheesecake

½ cup butter, softened

¼ cup packed brown sugar

1 cup all-purpose flour

¼ cup quick-cooking oats

¼ cup finely chopped pecans

½ teaspoon ground cinnamon

For crust, cream butter and brown sugar; Gradually add remaining ingredients until well blended. Press onto bottom and half way up the sides of a greased 9-inch springform pan. Place on a baking sheet, and bake at 325° for 10 minutes. Cool.

2 (8-ounce) packages cream cheese, softened

1 (14-ounce) can sweetened condensed milk

½ cup thawed apple juice concentrate

3 eggs, lightly beaten

Beat cream cheese until fluffy. Beat in milk and apple juice concentrate. Add eggs; beat on low speed just until combined (batter will be thin). Pour into crust. Bake, on baking sheet, at 325° for 40 to 45 minutes or until center is almost set. Cool 10 minutes. Carefully run a knife around edge of pan to loosen; cool another hour. Refrigerate overnight.

1 medium tart apple

¼ teaspoon ground cinnamon

Whole pecans

Cool Whip

Peel apple and slice very thin. Coat apple slices with cinnamon. As you cut the cheesecake, top each slice with apple slices, pecans and Cool Whip.

Local Favorite

Martin's Restaurant

1796 Carter Hill Road
Montgomery, AL 36106
334-265-1767
www.martinsrestaurant.org

Martin's Restaurant is a family-owned restaurant serving the Montgomery area for over 70 years. They offer a delicious home-style meal featuring the traditional meat-and-three plate for lunch and dinner. Though the menu changes daily, you will always find Martin's Famous Fried Chicken featuring the "pulley bone" every day. A large selection of delicious desserts includes Martin's homemade meringue pies as featured in "Travel and Leisure" magazine. Menu favorites include everything from baked turkey with dressing to homemade salmon croquettes, fried oysters to homemade chicken and dumplings. Martin's homemade cornbread muffins, featured in "Garden and Gun" magazine, are baked fresh every day from Martin's own recipe.

LUNCH
Sunday: 10:45 am to 2:45 pm
Monday – Friday: 11:00 am to 2:00 pm
DINNER
Monday – Friday: 2:00 pm to 7:30 pm

Paradise Salad

This is a Martin's favorite that is served every Monday.

1 (20-ounce) can strawberry pie filling

1 (20-ounce) can crushed pineapple, drained

1 (16-ounce) carton whipped topping

1 (8-ounce) carton sour cream

1 (14-ounce) can sweetened condensed milk

1 cup chopped nuts

Combine all ingredients and mix well. (You can also use cherry pie filling instead of strawberry.) Chill several hours before serving.

Restaurant Recipe

Sweet Potato Pie

Sweet Potato Pie is on our menu every Thursday. We prepare a lot of pies for Thanksgiving and this is one of our favorites.

4 cups cooked, mashed sweet potatoes

1½ cups firmly packed brown sugar

⅛ teaspoon salt

¾ cup butter, softened

4 eggs, separated

1 tablespoon vanilla extract

1 (12-ounce) can evaporated milk

1 (10-inch) unbaked pie shell

Combine sweet potatoes, brown sugar, salt and butter. Add egg yolks 1 at a time to potato mixture beating well after each addition. Add vanilla and mix. Add milk and mix. Beat egg whites until stiff. Fold into potato mixture. Pour into unbaked pie shell. Bake at 400° for 15 minutes. Reduce heat to 350° and bake 30 minutes.

Restaurant Recipe

Pineapple and Cheese Casserole

This is a Martin's favorite that is served every Tuesday.

2 (20-ounce) cans pineapple chunks in heavy syrup, undrained

1 cup sugar

5 tablespoons flour

1½ cups grated medium Cheddar cheese

1 sleeve Ritz crackers

1 stick butter, sliced thin

Preheat oven to 350°. Spray 9x13-inch glass pan with cooking spray. Pour pineapple (with juice) in pan. In a bowl, combine sugar and flour. Pour over pineapple. Sprinkle cheese on top. Crush crackers and spread over cheese. Place butter slices across casserole. Bake 30 to 45 minutes. Serve warm.

Restaurant Recipe

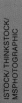

ISTOCK/THINKSTOCK/MSPHOTOGRAPHIC

HANK WILLIAMS MUSEUM
Montgomery, Alabama

Hank Williams, country music megastar, is Montgomery's most celebrated citizen. A life-size bronze statue of Hank wearing one of his flamboyant musical-note-embellished suits, strumming his guitar, and giving his famous tight-lipped smile stands across from Montgomery's City Hall. Be sure to visit the Hank Williams Museum where you can see, among many other things, Hank's "death car." And don't miss Hank's granite gravemarker embellished with musical notes, carvings of his guitar and boots, references to his most popular songs, and a sculpture of Hank's cowboy hat.

ON DISPLAY AT HANK WILLIAMS MUSEUM, MONTGOMERY

For more information, go to:
www.visitingmontgomery.com
www.thehankwilliamsmuseum.net

Sautéed Gator

14 ounces gator tail

Flour seasoned to taste

½ portabella mushroom, chopped

½ onion, chopped

½ green bell pepper, chopped

1 Roma tomato, chopped

1 tablespoon blackening season

⅛ cup white wine

⅛ cup Worcestershire sauce

Dust gator tail in flour, then deep fry about 20 seconds. Pan sauté mushroom, onion, bell pepper, tomato, blackening seasoning, white wine and Worcestershire sauce until vegetables are soft. Stir in gator; simmer approximately 2 to 3 minutes. Enjoy!

Restaurant Recipe

Frogz Restaurant

**711 East McKinnon Street
New Brockton, AL 36351
334-894-0033
www.frogzrestaurant.com**

Frogz Restaurant is a family-owned, family-operated business where the customer is, truly, the number one concern. Established in 2007, Frogz Restaurant was born of a desire to present the Wiregrass area with the highest quality food coupled with the greatest service experience delivered in a relaxed beach-like atmosphere. Frogz is a small restaurant that caters to the customer. If you desire something not on their menu, ask and they will try their best to accommodate your wishes. Talk about catering to the customer. They say, "Our goal is to make Frogz everyone's favorite restaurant."

**Wednesday – Saturday:
5:00 pm to 9:00 pm**

THINKSTOCK/ISTOCK/INGANEILSEN

Mike and Ed's BBQ

2001 Crawford Road
Phenix City, AL 36867
334-297-1012
www.mikeandedsbbq.com

In 1985, Mike Gullat and Ed Cook opened the first Mike & Ed's BBQ in Phenix City and have been serving the most delicious barbecue and home cooking favorites in the Southeast ever since. Now with five locations, it's even easier to enjoy their outstanding barbecue, great sides, and friendly service. You'll love the original location with its rustic feel featuring old signs, tin, and wood adorning the walls. Mike & Ed's is one of the best and most-loved barbecue restaurants in the South. Come on in and enjoy some good southern hospitality and the best barbecue around.

Monday – Saturday: 10:30 am to 9:00 pm

THINKSTOCK/FOGSTOCKRELEASE

Homemade
Peanut Butter Pie

1 (8-ounce) package cream cheese, softened

1 (8-ounce) jar extra-crunchy peanut butter

1½ cups powdered sugar

1 tablespoon vanilla extract

1 (12-ounce) carton Cool Whip

1 (9-inch) graham cracker crust

Combine all ingredients, except crust, in a bowl and mix well. Spread evenly in crust. Freeze to harden, 30 minutes or longer. When ready to serve, remove from freezer, cut and serve.

Restaurant Recipe

Pork Chop Sandwich

3 tablespoons salt

1⅓ cups lemon juice

1 (6- to 9-pound) boneless pork loin

**13th Street Bar-B-Q mild
barbecue sauce**

Mix salt and lemon juice in 16-ounce squirt bottle; fill with water. Cook pork loin, basting every 15 to 20 minutes with salted lemon water, over a wood fire for 2 to 2½ hours or until meat starts to firm up. Baste with barbecue sauce and wrap in foil. Place on grill away from direct heat for 1 to 1½ hours. Be prepared for some of the best pork chops you've ever eaten. To serve, slice pork loin in ½- to ¾-inch slices and serve on a bun with 13th Street Bar-B-Q Hot Sauce and BBQ Slaw.

Restaurant Recipe

13th Street Bar-B-Q

**1310 7th Avenue
Phenix City, AL 36867
334-291-1833**

13th Street Bar-B-Q opened August 26, 1988. All meats are slow cooked over an open wood fire. Definitely try their signature World Famous Pork Chop Sandwich and the almost famous Q-Tater. The menu also includes BBQ Pork Plates, Sandwiches, BBQ Chicken, Chef Salad, Smoked Ham & Turkey and mouth-watering St. Louis Style Ribs. **Accolades:** Alabama Public TV "Top 10 Best Places in Alabama," Alabama Department of Tourism's "100 Dishes to Eat in Alabama Before You Die" for the Pork Chop Sandwich, *Columbus* (GA) *Ledger Enquirer* "Readers Choice Award." 13th Street Bar-B-Q offers catering for any occasion and any size gathering.

**Wednesday & Saturday:
9:30 am to 3:00 pm
Monday, Tuesday, Thursday & Friday:
9:30 am to 6:00 pm
Closed Sunday**

Fat Boy's Bar-B-Que Ranch

154 First Street • Prattville, AL 36067
334-358-4227 • www.fatboysbarbqueranch.com

At Fat Boy's Bar-B-Que everything is homemade and the meats are slow cooked over natural hickory wood to accent the choice barbecue flavor of the South—"the way it's supposed to be." Owner Danny Loftin says it best, "After 25 years in the trucking and cattle business, Gretchen and I opened Fat Boy's Bar-B-Que Ranch in downtown Prattville on the banks of the Autauga Creek. When the opportunity came to open a restaurant I asked the Lord what he wanted me to do. After a lot of encouragement from friends and fervent prayers, the Lord simply said, 'Trust Me.' And I did. We leased a facility in 1998 and embarked on a new career for which we had no prior experience. In our restaurant of 52 seats, we opened on June 1 and suffered a fire 2½ months later. We remodeled and expanded the capacity to 75 seats and reopened in January 1999. A year later the restaurant was enlarged to a capacity of 175 with a new dining room and became established as an icon of local flavor where everything is homemade... 'the way it's supposed to be.' We purchased the building and an additional 1½ acres in 2004 to bring us to where we are now sitting on the creek bank. Our success is to the Glory of the Lord, not me or Gretchen."

Monday – Wednesday: 10:30 am to 2:30 pm
Thursday – Saturday: 10:30 am to 8:00 pm

Oreo Banana Split Pie

3 cups crushed Oreos

3 cups vanilla ice cream, softened

1½ cups sliced strawberries

1 (8-ounce) carton whipped topping

1 (3.9-ounce) box instant chocolate pudding prepared per package directions

2 bananas, sliced

Chocolate syrup for drizzling

2 tablespoons crushed dry-roasted peanuts

12 maraschino cherries

Spread Oreo crumbs in bottom of a 9-inch pie plate. Gently spoon ice cream over cookies and spread to an even layer. Layer strawberries over ice cream. In a separate bowl, combine whipped topping and pudding. Spread over strawberries. Top with banana slices then drizzle chocolate syrup over top. Sprinkle with nuts. Decorate top with cherries. Freeze at least 4 hours (or overnight), until completely firm. Allow to sit at room temperature for 5 minutes before slicing. Serves 8 to 10.

Family Favorite

All-In-One-Shop

**3000 Earl Goodwin Parkway
Selma, AL 36701
334-874-7002**

All-In-One-Shop should be your number one choice if you are looking for a home-away-from-home kind of restaurant. You'll feel right at home in the beautiful old-style house that is decorated to please. When it comes to great restaurants, it's always about the food, and you won't be disappointed in that department. No matter what you choose, the food is always superb and seasoned just right. If it's down home southern cooking that you love, there is only one place to look... All-In-One-Shop.

**Monday – Friday:
10:00 am to 3:00 pm
Sunday: 10:00 am to 5:00 pm**

Lannie's BBQ Spot

2115 Minter Avenue
Selma, AL 36703
334-874-4478

Lannie's is a family-owned, bare-bones, local, small-town dive. There are a few tables inside where family pictures adorn the wall, or you may get food to go. Either way, expect to be waited on by some of the nicest people you will ever have the pleasure of meeting. From pulled pork sandwiches to full plates of barbecue with the best sides you've ever eaten, visit Lannie's for the best barbecue in the state. You'll step back in time when you get to dessert. Lannie's desserts are just like grandmother made.

Monday – Thursday: 8:00 am to 8:00 pm
Friday – Saturday: 9:00 am to 8:00 pm

Old Fashioned Potato Pie

3 medium potatoes, peeled and diced

½ stick butter

Dash salt

1 cup sugar

2 eggs, well beaten

1 cup evaporated milk

1 teaspoon cinnamon

1 teaspoon vanilla extract

1 teaspoon ginger

1 teaspoon nutmeg

1 (9-inch) pie shell

Boil potatoes until tender; drain. Mash potatoes with butter, salt and sugar. Add eggs, milk and spices. Bake in pie shell at 350° for 45 minutes. Lower temperature to 300° and bake another 15 minutes until pie shell is brown on bottom.

Family Favorite

STURDIVANT HALL
Old Town Historic District
Selma, Alabama

Selma boasts the state's largest contiguous historic district, with over 1,250 structures including Sturdivant Hall. Construction on this beautiful former home was started in 1852. It became a museum in 1957 and assumed the name Sturdivant Hall. The museum contains period antique furnishings, porcelain and doll collections, as well as an impressive collection of art. A tour of this site includes the house, detached kitchen, gift shop, and formal garden. It is rumored that Sturdivant Hall is haunted by former owner John Parkman. A local banker who was imprisoned at the former Castle Morgan in Cahaba for cotton speculation, he was killed trying to escape.

For more information,
visit www.sturdivanthall.com.

Mark's Mart

1022 County Road 44
Selma, AL 36701
334-872-3003

Mark's Mart is a unique specialty foods market that has served the Selma and central Alabama area since 1980. The world-renowned Chicken Swirl® was invented here and worth the trip alone, but the steaks, beef or chicken kabobs, Cajun pork chops, and appetizers are amazing. Don't forget the twice-baked potatoes. Add a homemade cake or pie, and you've made a meal to remember! We might also suggest choosing from their amazing selection of fine wines and craft beer. Locally made cheese straws, Amish cheeses, or Southern Ambrosia Honey, are just a few of the must-haves this one-stop shop has to offer. Well worth the special trip or leisurely drive on a Sunday afternoon!

Monday – Thursday: 7:00 am to 8:00 pm
Friday & Saturday: 7:00 am to 8:30 pm
Sunday: 3:30 pm to 7:00 pm

Grilled Chicken Swirls with Bacon Wrapped Asparagus

4 Chicken Swirls®
Southern Flavor Charbroil Seasoning
Salt and pepper
1 pound sliced smoked bacon
2 bunches fresh asparagus
Pilleteri's Liquid Marinade

Lightly coat Chicken Swirls with Southern Flavor Charbroil Seasoning, salt and pepper to taste. Cut smoked bacon slices in half. Cut ends from asparagus. Wrap asparagus, in bunches of 3 to 4, with smoked bacon. Season to taste with salt, pepper and Southern Flavor Charbroil Seasoning. Grill chicken and asparagus, basting frequently with Pilleteri's Liquid Marinade. Remove chicken when it is cooked through. Remove asparagus when they are good and hot, but still crunchy.

Note: All items for this recipe are available at Mark's Mart.

Restaurant Recipe

THINKSTOCK/ISTOCK/HOANGPHOTO

Fried Cornbread

1 teaspoon granulated onion

1 cup chopped onion

5 cups cornmeal

2 cups flour

3 eggs, beaten

2⅔ cups milk

Heat grease to 350° in deep-fat fryer. Combine first 4 ingredients in a large mixing bowl. Stir in eggs and milk, using additional milk if necessary. Drop by spoonful into hot grease and fry until golden brown.

Restaurant Recipe

Mossy Grove Schoolhouse Restaurant

1841 Alabama Highway 87
Troy, AL 36079
334-566-4921

Mossy Grove Schoolhouse is a restaurant with history. The original deed to the school trustees was signed December 16, 1856. When you enter the restaurant, you are standing in the original one-room schoolhouse. The large dining room on the north was added in 1917. The stage, upon which many plays were produced and from which the teacher directed the class, has been left intact in the back dining room. This historic, southern atmosphere, plus excellent food, is a combination sure to make your visit to Mossy Grove Schoolhouse Restaurant an unforgettable pleasure.

Tuesday – Saturday: 5:00 pm to 9:00 pm

Hilltop Grill

18627 Highway 82
Union Springs, AL 36089
334-738-3000

Hilltop Grill is one of the oldest, continuously operating businesses in Union Springs. Originally established 1951, generations of Bullock County natives grew up with Ms. Rhodes's hamburgers, cheeseburgers, barbecue sandwiches, and a heaping side of good, old-fashioned, small-town fat chewing. The newest owner, Rebekah Tompkins Johnson, has been in foodservice for over 30 years and is a lifelong resident of Bullock County and grew up stopping by The Grill. She has revamped the menu to include more fresh, hand-prepared items, introduced new catering ideas like her take home and bake casseroles, from scratch desserts and Beck's cheesestraws —a local favorite.

Monday – Friday: 6:00 am to 3 pm
Saturday: 6:00 am to 2:00 pm

Garlic Cheese Bread

This is a recipe from my daughter Farrar Foley. It's the most delicious bread EVER.

3½ cups shredded Cheddar cheese

¾ cup shredded Monterey Jack cheese

½ cup grated Parmesan cheese

½ cup mayonnaise

4 green onions, minced (white and green parts)

Dash salt

1 loaf French bread

1 stick butter

4 cloves garlic, finely minced

Preheat oven to 425°. Mix cheeses with mayonnaise and green onions. Add salt to taste. Cut loaf in half lengthwise, then cut in half so loaf is in quarters. Melt 2 tablespoons butter in skillet and add 1 garlic clove. Place 1 of the quarter loaves face down in the skillet, swirling it to soak up the butter and garlic. Allow bread to toast in the skillet (remove garlic if it starts to get too brown). Repeat until all bread, butter and garlic are used. Spread cheese mixture on warm loaves and bake until cheese is hot and bubbly, about 10 minutes. Slice and serve.

Family Favorite

Red Velvet Cake

½ cup shortening

1½ cups sugar

2 eggs

2¼ cups plain flour

2 teaspoons cocoa

1 teaspoon baking soda

1 teaspoon salt

1 teaspoon vinegar

¼ cup (2 ounces) red food coloring

1 cup buttermilk

1 teaspoon vanilla extract

Cream shortening and sugar; add eggs and mix well. Sift together flour, cocoa, baking soda and salt. Mix vinegar and food coloring. Add flour mixture to sugar mixture alternately with buttermilk mixing well. Stir in food coloring mixture. Add vanilla; beat until well blended. Divide batter between 3 treated 8-inch round cake pans. Bake at 350° for 35 minutes. Do not overbake. Cool.

Cream Cheese Icing:

1 stick butter, softened

1 (8-ounce) package cream cheese, softened

1 (16-ounce) box powdered sugar

1½ teaspoons vanilla extract

1 cup chopped pecans

Mix all together; spread on cooled cake.

Restaurant Recipe

1953 BBQ Sauce

1 gallon ketchup

6 cups brown sugar

1 gallon tomato juice

½ cup black pepper

4 cups white vinegar

Mix altogether well. Keep refrigerated.

Restaurant Recipe

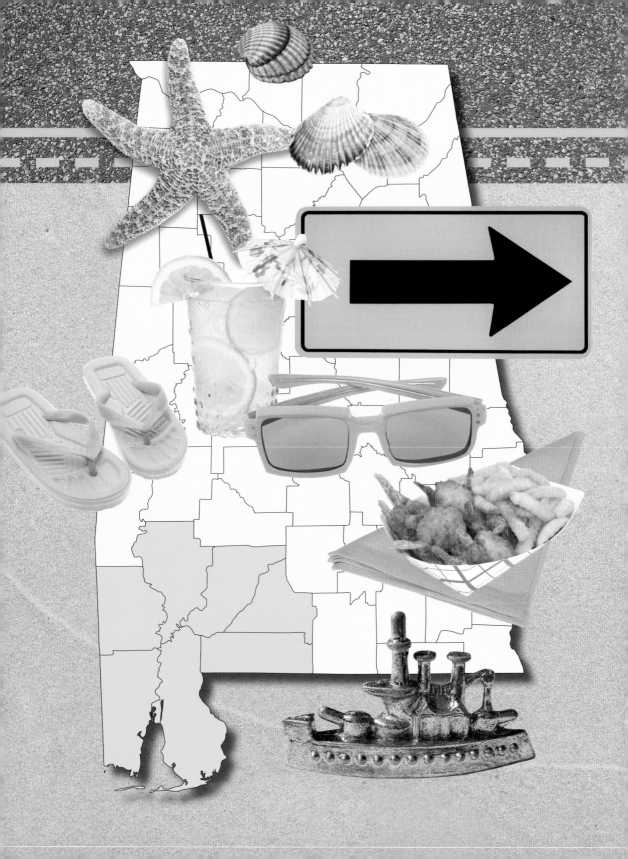

Gulf Coast REGION

Street's Seafood Restaurant

251 Highway 31 South
Bay Minette, AL 36507
251-937-2664 • 251-937-4096

Street's Seafood Restaurant is a family-owned, family-operated restaurant that has been serving the area 40 years. Their country-style breakfast is the best way to start the day. At lunch, there is a country-style buffet with great-tasting fresh food and something to please everyone. The menu includes a wide variety from po' boys to hamburgers to seafood platters. Their shrimp and fried crab claws are a local favorite. On weekends, the all-you-can-eat seafood buffet is super-popular, so get there early. Whatever you do, don't miss Street's banana pudding. As their sign says, "Street's Restaurant. If you missed us, you wasted your trip."

Monday – Sunday: 5:00 am to 9:00 pm

Street's Chicken Salad

Voted Alabama's Best

4 cups cooked, finely shredded fresh chicken breast

2 hard-boiled eggs, chopped

3 ribs celery, chopped

1 cup mayonnaise

Salt and pepper to taste

Combine all ingredients and mix well. Refrigerate overnight or until ready to serve. Serve over a lettuce leaf with grapes, strawberries and apples on the side.

Restaurant Recipe

Blueberry Pie

1 (3-ounce) box grape Jell-O

¾ cup boiling water

4 to 5 ice cubes

3 cups fresh blueberries, washed

1 (15-ounce) can blueberry pie filling

1 (16-ounce) carton Cool Whip

2 shortbread or graham cracker
pie crusts

Combine Jell-O with boiling water; stir until dissolved. Add ice cubes. When ice is melted, add blueberries and pie filling. Mix well. Pour into pie crusts. Top with Cool Whip and a few fresh blueberries.

Restaurant Recipe

Bobby's Fish Camp

686 Bobby's Camp Road
Silas, AL 36919
251-754-9225

One of the oldest restaurants in southwest Alabama, Bobby's Fish Camp was started by Bobby Dahlberg in 1956. Since his death in 2011, Lora Jane McIlwain carries on the traditions started by her father. Travel back in time to eat the best catfish served in Alabama and read about all the happenings in the area from long ago days—like the explosion of the James T. Staples river boat and how it came to rest in front of the camp. Stay at one of the two RV sites or rent a cabin. Dock your boat alongside the yachts that come through from all over the word or launch your boat right at the camp. Check out the museum and sign the guestbook having your name alongside people from Brazil, Germany, Norway, and Canada. You never know who you will run into at Bobby's Fish Camp.

Thursday – Friday: 3:00 pm to 9:00 pm
Saturday: 12:00 pm to 9:00 pm
Sunday: 12:00 pm to 6:00 pm

LeJeune's Market by the Bay

29145 US Highway 98
Daphne, AL 36526
251-621-9664
www.marketbythebay.com

LeJeune's Market by the Bay has been a fixture of the Eastern Shore since opening its doors in 2004. Family-owned and operated, LeJeune's is dedicated to offering the best Gulf seafood available as well as serving mouthwatering shrimp po' boys, fried oysters, fish, and gumbo all served up with the best customer service around. Drop by, say "Hi," and set a spell. At LeJeune's, they'll love getting to know you.

FRESH SEAFOOD MARKET & RESTAURANT
Sunday & Monday: 11:00 am to 3:00 pm
Tuesday – Saturday: 11:00 am to 7:00 pm

Crabmeat Pie

This is a rich and delicious taste of the best the Gulf Coast has to offer.

3 tablespoons minced green onion

1 tablespoon minced red bell pepper

3 tablespoons butter

½ pound crabmeat

3 eggs, beaten

¾ cup half-and-half

1 cup shredded cheese

Salt, Tabasco, pepper, Old Bay and Worcestershire sauce to taste

1 (9-inch) unbaked pie shell

Gently combine all ingredients, except pie shell. Place in unbaked pie shell. Bake at 375° for 45 minutes or until a knife inserted comes out clean.

Family Favorite

Crabmeat Stuffing for Flounder

2 tablespoons each minced celery, red bell pepper and green onion

3 tablespoons butter, divided

½ cup Italian breadcrumbs

2 teaspoons Old Bay seasoning (or your favorite seafood seasoning)

1 to 2 dashes Tabasco

1 teaspoon Worcestershire sauce

2 tablespoons mayonnaise

1 pound lump crabmeat

4 flounders, medium size

Salt and pepper

Sauté celery, bell pepper and green onion in 1 tablespoon butter until tender crisp. Add breadcrumbs, Old Bay, Tabasco, Worcestershire, mayonnaise and crabmeat; mix well. Cover and refrigerate at least 1 hour. Place a quarter of the stuffing in each flounder pouch. (Your fish monger will gladly cut a side pouch for you or slit the flounders back to produce two pockets for stuffing.) Drizzle each with ½ tablespoon butter. Salt and pepper outside of flounder to taste. Spray a shallow baking pan. Place fish in pan. Cover and bake in 375° oven for 25 minutes or until fish flakes very easily with a fork. Remove cover; bake another 5 minutes.

Owners Victor, Robin, and Chad LeJeune are shown here with the fresh catch of the day—shrimp. At LeJeune's, we sell the freshest seafood we can find at the market, and also prepare and serve it fresh daily in the restaurant.

Note: This recipe is amazingly simple and versatile. It makes a great topping for baked fish fillets or for the more adventurous it can be spread over a fish fillet and rolled. Leftover stuffing can be converted into crab cakes or frozen for later use.

Family Favorite

The Lighthouse Bakery

919 Chaumont Avenue
Dauphin Island, AL 36528
251-861-2253
www.facebook.com/LighthouseBakery

The Lighthouse Bakery, owned and operated by Mary and Daniel Scarcliff for more than 15 years, is the place to go for breakfast on Dauphin Island. Fresh-ground coffee, mouth-watering pastries, and tasty omelets served with a smile in a house over 100 years old all make a visit to The Lighthouse Bakery an experience you won't want to miss. Stop by for lunch and bite into a deli sandwich on freshly baked breads and rolls, then order up a homemade pie or cake to take home. Try it once and it will be a favorite forever.

Wednesday – Friday: 6:00 am to 3:00 pm
Saturday: 6:00 am to 4:00 pm
Sunday: 9:00 am to 3:00 pm

Strawberry Pecan Muffins

3 cups unbleached flour
1 teaspoon baking soda
1 teaspoon ground cinnamon
1 teaspoon salt
Dash freshly ground nutmeg, optional
1 cup canola oil
3 eggs, beaten
2 cups sugar
4 cups chopped strawberries
1 cup freshly chopped pecans, optional

Streusel Topping, optional:

1 cup sugar
¾ cup flour
¼ cup butter

Preheat oven 350°. Combine first 5 (dry) ingredients; set aside. Combine oil, eggs and sugar; mix until creamy. Add dry ingredients, mixing just until moistened. Stir in strawberries and pecans by hand. Measure into greased and floured muffin tins to two-thirds full. Top with Streusel Topping, if desired. Bake until toothpick comes out clean, 20 to 25 minutes.

Restaurant Recipe

Corn and Crab Bisque

½ pound butter

½ pound (about 2 cups) flour

4 cups chicken or vegetable stock

¾ cup minced onion

1 tablespoon minced garlic

1 (15.5-ounce) can cream-style corn

3 quarts heavy whipping cream

Thyme to taste

1 bay leaf

2 pounds Gulf blue crabmeat

Salt and pepper to taste

Chopped chives or lemon grass
for garnish

Make blonde roux by melting butter in skillet and stirring in flour until well combined. Cook until roux is a very light brown; set aside. Bring stock to a boil; add onion, garlic and corn. Return to a boil and whisk in roux. Thin to desired thickness with heavy whipping cream. Reduce heat to low simmer; add the thyme and bay leaf. Add crabmeat and season to taste. Cook just until heated through. Garnish with fresh chopped chives or lemon grass.

Restaurant Recipe

The Common Loon Café

**100 Florida Street
East Brewton, AL 36426
251-809-6009**

Family owned and family operated, The Common Loon focuses on local, wild-caught Gulf of Mexico or USA domestic seafood. The menu is based around fresh, top-grade ingredients with generous portions at a price that is unmatched. Their seafood gumbo and corn and crab bisque are family recipes created in-house by the father and son team who cook there. Once a week, The Common Loon Café hosts "Soup Line Sunday" when the chef serves a special soup, free of charge, to the needy and hungry. The Common Loon Café is a simple, low-key seafood café where you'll enjoy topnotch seafood from people who have a heart to serve.

**Monday – Thursday: 11:00 am to 3:00 pm
Friday & Saturday: 11:00 am to 7:00 pm**

Pirates Cove Marina & Restaurant

6664 County Road 95 • Elberta, AL 36530
251-987-1224 • www.piratescoveriffraff.com

Pirates Cove is a come-as-you-are unique restaurant located in the Josephine community overlooking Arnica Bay and Roberts Bayou. The restaurant has been in the Mueller family for 56 years and is known for cheeseburgers, pizzas, and bushwhackers. The burgers are one-third pound, certified Angus ground chuck dressed with a secret Cove Sauce, lettuce, tomato, and grilled onions. A local favorite is the pizza made with Pirates Cove's special dough recipe. Pirates Cove hosts the Pirates

Cove Wood Boat Festival in early May, the Illuminating Autism FUNraiser in early June, and the Cove Dog Olympics in mid-October.

**Open 7 days week
for breakfast, lunch & dinner**

Pizza Dough

5 pounds high-gluten flour

8 ounces (½ pound) white cornmeal

3 tablespoons salt

20 ounces (2½ cups) hot water

4 tablespoons sugar

4 tablespoons brown sugar

2 (12-ounce) bottles Black and Tan beer, cold

1¾ tablespoons active dry yeast

4 ounces olive oil

Blend flour, cornmeal and salt together in a large mixing bowl. In a separate bowl, blend hot water, sugar and brown sugar until sugars are dissolved. One at a time, stirring well after each addition, add beer, yeast and oil to hot water mixture. Set aside until yeast is bubbling nicely, about 15 minutes. Add to flour mixture and blend. Knead until flour is fully incorporated. Let dough rise for at least 1 hour. Divide into 8 dough balls. Each ball will make 1 (14-inch) pizza.

Restaurant Recipe

Bushwacker

1 part Malibu Coconut Rum

1 part Kahlúa (coffee liqueur)

2 parts vanilla ice cream

6 parts water/ice

1 jigger 151 Rum

Place Malibu Rum, Kahlúa, ice cream, and water/ice in blender and blend until smooth. Top with 151 Rum.

Restaurant Recipe

Big Daddy's Grill

16542 Ferry Road
Fairhope, Al 36532
www.bigdaddysgrill.net
251-990-8555

Big Daddy's Grill is a casual, river-front family restaurant offering friendly, full service with a full bar all year long. Known for fresh local shrimp, crab claws, and oysters, Big Daddy's also serves great hamburgers, chicken, salads, appetizers, and homemade desserts. The family-friendly environment offers two large sand piles for children while mom and dad enjoy the view and their food.

Take a virtual tour of Big Daddy's Grill at http://rtvpix.com/RT-0218-ZYOYIW-01.

Monday – Saturday: 11:00 am to 9:00 pm
Sunday: 11:00 am to 8:00 pm
LIVE MUSIC
Year around: every Friday night from 5:00 pm to 9:00 pm
March – October
Saturdays: 4:00 pm to 8:00 pm • Sundays: 3:00 pm to 7:00 pm

Spinach Dip

At home my wife scoops out a loaf of Hawaiian bread to make a bread bowl and fills it with the dip.

1 pound frozen chopped spinach, thawed and drained

2 cups mayonnaise

1 cup sour cream

3 (1.4-ounce) packages Knorr's vegetable soup mix

2 cups shredded Jack/Cheddar cheese

Combine all ingredients. This dip can be served cold or heated. Serve with tortilla chips or any kind of cracker you enjoy.

Family Recipe

Rémoulade Sauce

2 cups mayonnaise

1 cup horseradish

¼ cup Worcestershire sauce

2 tablespoons lemon juice

Paprika

Tabasco

Combine mayonnaise, horseradish, Worcester-shire and lemon juice. Add paprika for color to light pink (not too much; color shouldn't be red or orange). Stir in Tabasco sauce to taste (we add a lot). We serve this sauce with our crawfish tails and our crab cakes but it is great on any seafood.

Restaurant Recipe

The Biscuit King Café

LARRY DYESS, URBANSPOON.COM

9501 County Road 24
Fairhope, AL 36532
251-928-2424

Opened 18 years ago, The Biscuit King Café is family owned by Willie and Nancy Foster and was started with Willie working tirelessly to perfect a biscuit better than one his wife makes. He ended up with the perfect biscuit that has everything baked inside—bacon, sausage, egg, and cheese. These days anything goes for this unique biscuit which may even include blueberries, strawberries, and bananas. With a full breakfast menu and a lunch menu that includes country cooking, blue plate specials, barbecue, burgers, and sandwiches, Biscuit King offers a down-home experience served up by a friendly staff.

7 days a week: 5:00 am to 2:00 pm

Old Fashioned Meatloaf

Meatloaf:

5 pounds ground beef

5 eggs, beaten

2 cups breadcrumbs

½ cup minced onion

1 tablespoon pepper

1 tablespoon salt

1 tablespoon minced garlic

½ tablespoon spaghetti seasoning

¾ cup Worcestershire sauce

½ cup milk

¾ cup ketchup

Topping:

Ketchup

1 pound bacon

Combine meatloaf ingredients and mix well. Shape into 4 loaves and place in a baking pan about 2 inches apart. Bake at 350° for 30 minutes. Cover each loaf with ketchup then strips of bacon. Bake another 10 minutes or until no longer pink in the center.

Restaurant Recipe

Cornbread

½ stick butter

1½ cups self-rising flour

1½ cups cornmeal

¼ cup sugar

2 eggs, beaten

1 teaspoon baking powder

Buttermilk

Preheat oven to 400°. Place butter in 11x7-inch pan and put in oven while heating. Combine remaining ingredients, except buttermilk, in a bowl. Add buttermilk, a little at a time, mixing after each addition until mixture reaches the consistency of cake-mix batter. Pour into hot pan. Bake 15 minutes or until fully set and golden brown.

Restaurant Recipe

Peach Cobbler

1 stick butter

2 cups Bisquick

2 cups sugar

2 cups milk

2 (29-ounce) cans sliced peaches in heavy syrup

Preheat oven to 400°. Place butter in a 12x17-inch baking pan and place pan in oven while heating. Blend dry ingredients with milk and pour in hot pan when butter is melted. Drain and discard about half the juice from peaches. Carefully pour peaches and remaining juice over batter in pan. Bake until firm, about 60 to 75 minutes.

Restaurant Recipe

THINKSTOCK/ISTOCK/JACK PUCCIO

Old 27 Grill

**19992 Highway 181
(Old County Road 27)
Fairhope, AL 36532
251-281-2663
www.old27grill.com**

Old 27 Grill is a casual dining, family-friendly restaurant and grocery, offering 27 beers and wines and 27 toppings for the best hamburgers, hot dogs, and steaks on the Eastern Shore. Fresh and local means a great deal at Old 27 Grill; they use fresh, locally-baked rolls, produce that comes from the region when in season, and hand cut the steaks and patty the burgers fresh every day. Visit Old 27 Grill to relax with family and friends, laugh a little at the acorns hitting the tin roof, and let them serve you for a great experience that will make you one of the locals.

Monday – Friday: 11:00 am to 9:00 pm
Saturday: 10:30 am to 9:30 pm
Sunday: 10:30 am to 8:00 pm

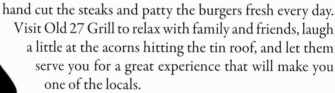

Ecor Rouge Catch

An Old 27 Grill signature dish

Fish:

1 (7- to 9-ounce) mild white fish fillet
(tilapia, pangisius or catfish)

1 cup all-purpose flour

1 teaspoon salt

1 teaspoon cayenne pepper

2 teaspoons paprika

1 egg

2 cups milk

Sift flour and seasonings together in a dry bowl. In a separate bowl, beat egg with a fork into milk to prepare an egg wash. Dredge fish in dry flour mixture, then egg wash, then once again in flour mixture. Place fish directly into fryer at 350° and fry for 4 to 6 minutes (will be ready once floating). Try to time the frying of the fish so that it is done at the same time your sauce is completed.

Sauce:

1 ounce (2 tablespoons) melted butter

2 large peeled shrimp
(16 to 20 count works best)

½ ounce (1 tablespoon) dry vermouth

½ cup heavy whipping cream

1 dash cayenne pepper

2 dashes paprika

2 tablespoons chopped green onion

1 lemon wheel (slice of lemon
on the circle)

Melt butter and in a sauté pan. Add shrimp and vermouth. Turn shrimp once and add heavy cream. Add cayenne and paprika and allow sauce to reduce by half. Sprinkle green onions into sauce.

Place fish fillet in the center of your dish. Lay shrimp on the top of fish and drizzle sauce over fish to allow for good plate coverage. Garnish with a fresh lemon wheel and serve immediately.

Restaurant Recipe

THINKSTOCK/ISTOCK/PEDRO GUILLERMO ANGELES-FLORES

Lemon Cream Cheese Pound Cake

3 cups sugar

1¼ cups butter

1 (8-ounce) package cream cheese, softened

1 tablespoon lemon juice

1 teaspoon vanilla extract

1 teaspoon lemon extract

½ teaspoon orange extract

⅛ teaspoon salt

6 eggs

3 cups cake flour

Beat sugar, butter and cream cheese until fluffy. Beat in lemon juice, vanilla, lemon extract, orange extract and salt. Add eggs 1 at a time beating after each addition. Add flour, and beat until smooth. Pour batter in greased and floured tube or Bundt pan. Bake at 325° for 1½ hours or until golden brown. Cool 10 minutes. Remove from pan. Cool cake completely. Pour Lemon Glaze over cake and serve.

Lemon Glaze:

1 cup powdered sugar

1 tablespoon softened butter

2 teaspoons grated lemon rind

2 to 3 tablespoons lemon juice

Mix all ingredients until smooth using 2 tablespoons lemon juice; add additional lemon juice if needed.

Local Favorite

Down South BBQ

County Road 10
Foley, AL 36535
251-955-6622

The name Down South BBQ evokes thoughts of warm southern days, friendly people, the smell of smoking meat soon to be served up with delicious, freshly-made coleslaw, and delicious sweets just like grandma made. This is exactly what you get when you come to Down South BBQ which has been in business for more than seven years and is family owned and family operated. A local favorite is their cornbread sandwich made with two pancakes, either regular or jalapeño, a mound of pork, and sauce with homemade slaw on top. YUM!

Tuesday – Friday: 10:00 am to 6:30 pm
Saturday: 10:00 am to 4:00 pm

Apple Cheese

A famous Gift Horse recipe

3 dozen cooking apples, peeled, cored and sliced

52 ounces Cheddar cheese, grated

4 cups flour

4 sleeves Ritz crackers, crumbled

4 cups sugar

2 cups margarine, melted

Simmer apples in boiling water until tender. Remove from water; drain. Using a quarter of the apples, divided evenly and place a layer in each of 3 buttered 9x13-inch casserole dishes. Combine remaining ingredients. Using about a quarter of the mixture, sprinkle evenly over apples in each pan. Repeat layering until all ingredients are used. Bake at 350° for 35 to 45 minutes.

Restaurant Recipe

The Gift Horse Restaurant

209 West Laurel Avenue
Foley, AL 36535
251-943-3663

Foley's only landmark restaurant offers a unique dining experience in a grand, old 1912 building with beaded pine walls and ceilings. It is open for the enjoyment and merriment of people who enjoy dining in complete luxury, yet in a casual atmosphere. The Gift Horse Restaurant offers a traditional buffet specializing in scrumptious southern cuisine—fried and baked chicken, praline sweet potatoes, apple cheese, fried biscuits that melt in your mouth, and seafood gumbo are just a few items on the "groaning" buffet table. Enjoy and experience the southern hospitality of The Gift Horse Restaurant—you'll be glad you did.

7 days a week: 11:00 am to 8:00 pm

FOLEY DEPOT MUSEUM
Foley, Alabama

The museum is housed in the old Louisville and Nashville Railroad Station. Built in 1908, it was sold for a dollar in 1971 and moved five miles to another city, then deeded to the city of Foley and moved back to its original location where it became Foley Depot Museum. There you can see photos, tools, and memorabilia documenting Foley history and the important role the railroad played in developing the area. It is part of the Foley Railroad Station which also includes an "O" Gauge train exhibit complete with multiple engines, trains, and a quarter mile of track

a 1940 L&N diesel locomotive, caboose, and boxcar; plus a little train that will take you on a ride around Foley's Heritage Park.

For more information, visit www.visitfoley.org

Fried Potatoes & Onions

3 cups vegetable (or canola) oil

5 pounds potatoes, sliced ¼-inch thick

1 pound white onions, julienne

¼ cup Lambert's Fried Potato Seasoning

Place 3 cups oil in pan and heat to 425°. Place a single slice of potato in oil to see if it is hot enough to fry. Add potatoes to oil. Add onions on top. Add seasoning. Cover and cook 5 minutes, without stirring (bottom of potatoes will be brown). Flip and cook another 5 minutes or to your desired "crunch." You're done. Enjoy!

Restaurant Recipe

Lambert's Café

2981 South McKenzie
Foley, AL 36535
251-943-7655
www.throwedrolls.com

Lambert's Café opened in 1942. For more than 70 years they have entertained visitors with great home-style cooked meals in a roaring atmosphere. On a busy day in 1976, Norman Lambert was handing out rolls in the crowded restaurant. He couldn't reach a patron in the back, so the man yelled, "Just thrown the @#*^ thing!" And he did. That is how Lambert's Café began throwing rolls. Visit Lambert's Café today— like Norman used to say, "come eat or we'll both starve." In addition to Foley, Alabama, visit their other locations in Sikeston, Missouri, and Ozark, Missouri.

7 days a week: 10:30 am to 9:00 pm

Hope's Cheesecake

210 East 20th Avenue
Gulf Shores, AL 36542
888.968.4673
www.hopescheesecake.com

Hope's Cheesecake has been a Gulf Coast favorite since 1996. Hope's features gourmet desserts and is staffed by bakers with more than 30 years' baking experience. They make the best and most delicious desserts—cheesecakes, cupcakes, and a variety of other desserts—money can buy and deliver them to you "dinner party ready." Each gourmet cheesecake has a delicious, unique crust. They are made in small batches with only the finest ingredients like Kraft Philadelphia cream cheese, fresh whole eggs, pure cane sugar, and juice squeezed from fresh lemons. Stop by the store or shop online, but definitely try one of Hope's delicious cheesecakes.

Monday – Sunday: 10:00 am to 10:00 pm

Our Best Cheesecake

**1¾ cups Honey Maid
graham cracker crumbs**

⅓ cup margarine or butter, melted

1¼ cups sugar, divided

**3 (8-ounce) packages Philadelphia
cream cheese, softened**

**1 cup Breakstones or
Knudsen sour cream**

2 teaspoons vanilla extract

3 eggs

1 (21-ounce) can cherry pie filling

Preheat oven to 350° (if using silver pan; 325° if using dark nonstick pan). Mix graham cracker crumbs, margarine and ¼ cup sugar. Press firmly onto bottom and 2½ inches up side of 8- or 9-inch springform pan; set aside.

Beat cream cheese and remaining 1 cup sugar in large bowl with electric mixer on medium speed until well blended. Add sour cream and vanilla; mix well. Add eggs, 1 at a time, beating on low speed after each addition just until blended. Pour into crust.

Bake 60 to 70 minutes or until center is almost set. Turn oven off, and open oven door slightly. Let cheesecake set in oven 1 hour. Remove cheesecake from oven; cool completely. Refrigerate at least 4 hours or overnight. Loosen cheesecake from rim of pan; remove rim. Top cheesecake with pie filling just before serving. Store leftover cheesecake in refrigerator.

How to easily cut creamy desserts:

When cutting creamy-textured desserts such as cheesecake, carefully wipe off the knife blade between cuts with a clean damp towel. This prevents the creamy filling from building up on the blade, ensuring nice clean cuts that leave the filling intact.

Restaurant Recipe

The Original Oyster House

Celebrating 30 years!

www.OriginalOysterHouse.com

AT THE BEACH
701 Highway 59 South • Gulf Shores, AL 36542
251-948-2445

ON THE BAY
3733 Battleship Parkway • Mobile, AL 36527
251-626-2188

In May of 1983, the first Original Oyster House opened its doors in Gulf Shores. Not only is it the oldest seafood restaurant on Pleasure Island, it is nestled in the Original Oyster House Boardwalk—the area's oldest specialty shopping center. The Original Oyster House on the Mobile Bay Causeway opened in 1985.

The goal since 1983, in understanding the importance of family, has been to exceed customer expectations. The staff at The Original Oyster House takes pride in offering guests a selection of local and regional seafood. The delicious seafood gumbo is made fresh daily, using the finest ingredients available.

Visit them online for location hours: www.OriginalOysterHouse.com

Chocolate Chip Peanut Butter Pie

1 (8-ounce) package cream cheese, chilled

1 cup peanut butter, chilled

1 tablespoon Kahlúa

1/2 (16-ounce) box powdered sugar

1 (16-ounce) carton whipped topping

¾ cup miniature chocolate chips

1 (9-inch) Oreo pie shell

Mix cream cheese, peanut butter, Kahlúa and powdered sugar together. Add whipped topping and blend well. Fold in chocolate chips. Pour into pie shell. It should be mounded high in middle. Refrigerate until ready to serve. Serve with a dollop of whipped cream, if desired.

Restaurant Recipe

Lighthouse Restaurant

12495 Padgett Switch Road
Irvington, AL 36544
251-824-2500

Lighthouse Restaurant is a nice, southern, family restaurant decorated in nautical décor. Friendly waitresses and an attentive staff greet you and make you feel at home. With seating for 100 to 125 people, Lighthouse Restaurant can accommodate benefits and rehearsal dinners and even wedding receptions. They offer delicious, home-cooked meals Monday through Saturday.

Monday – Saturday: 11:00 am to 9:00 pm

Crawfish Casserole

1 cup finely chopped onion
1 cup finely chopped celery
1 cup finely chopped bell pepper
3 gloves garlic
1 stick butter
2 pounds crawfish tails
1 (10-ounce) can cream of mushroom soup
1 (10-ounce) can cream of shrimp soup
Salt and pepper
2 cups cooked rice, cooked
1 cup water
1 cup chopped parsley
1 cup chopped green onion tops
2 cups crushed breadcrumbs

Sauté onion, celery, bell pepper and garlic in butter until vegetables are soft. Add 2 pounds crawfish tails; cook 4 minutes. Add cream of mushroom soup and cream of shrimp soup; season to taste with salt and pepper. Add rice, water, parsley and green onion. Heat thoroughly, pour into casserole pan and sprinkle with breadcrumbs. Bake 25 minutes at 375°. (You may add shrimp and crabmeat to make this a seafood casserole.) Serves around 50.

Restaurant Recipe

Crawfish Étouffée

1 stick butter

1 hot pepper, chopped

1 large onion, chopped

1 small bell pepper, chopped

½ cup chopped celery

2 cloves garlic, minced

2 tablespoons flour

1 pound crawfish tails, peeled

Salt and pepper to taste

¼ cup chopped parsley

¼ cup finely chopped green onion top

Melt butter in a heavy gauge pot. Sauté hot pepper, onion, bell pepper, celery and garlic in butter until soft. Add flour; cook, stirring quickly, until golden brown. Add crawfish tails, salt and pepper. Add 1 cup water or fish stock and bring to a boil. Lower temperature and cook 10 minutes. Add parsley and onion tops; cook 5 minutes. Serve over rice and enjoy.

Restaurant Recipe

THINKSTOCK/ISTOCK/SIXTY7A

A Lil' Touch of Cajun Grill

207 South Kimball Avenue
Jackson, AL 36545
251-246-2993

Are you looking for "A Lil' Touch of Cajun?" We have the place for you. At A Lil' Touch of Cajun Grill you will enjoy a warm country atmosphere with Cajun music playing in the background and frequent live music. With a different special every night, you enjoy five-star food without the five-star cost. From southern-style Meatloaf to a perfectly seasoned Philly Toaster, from Crawfish Pie to Deep Fried Steak, from BBQ Ribs to Fish & Grits, meals are always unique and always delicious.

Monday – Thursday:
11:00 am to Midnight
Friday – Saturday: 11:00 am to 1:00 am
Sunday: 11:00 am to 8:00 pm

Shrimp Étouffée

2 tablespoons Cajun seasoning

2 tablespoons minced garlic

1 stick butter

1 (10-ounce) can Rotel tomatoes

1 (8-ounce) package cream cheese

1 (10-ounce) can cream of celery soup

1 (10-ounce) can cream of mushroom soup

2 to 3 pounds shrimp, peeled

Salt, pepper and cayenne pepper to taste

Sauté Cajun seasoning and garlic in butter. Add Rotel and sauté 2 more minutes. Add cream cheese; cook and stir until melted. Add both soups and cook about 30 minutes, stirring occasionally. Add shrimp and season to taste with salt, pepper and cayenne. Cook just until shrimp are done, 3 to 5 minutes.

Restaurant Recipe

HENRY STUART COTTAGE
Fairhope, Alabama

This small, round, hurricane-proof hut is made of concrete and was built by Henry Stuart who moved to Fairhope in the 1920's after being told by his doctor that he had only a year to live. Perpetually barefoot and sporting a long white beard, Stuart was known as the Hermit of Montrose. He lived in this hut 18 years before eventually moving on. He died at age 88. The hut, dubbed "Tolstoy Park" by local author Sonny Brewer, has become an unusual tourist attraction, writing sanctuary, meditation place, and shrine to eccentricity and individualism.

Burris Farm Market

3100 South Hickory Street
Loxley, AL 36551
251-964-6464

Burris Farm Market is a family-owned and operated open-air farmers market and bakery that has served both its town of Loxley and the greater Baldwin/Mobile County area since its establishment in 1986. In addition to fresh and local produce, the Burris Farm Market Bakery prepares freshly baked goods daily including breads, cobblers and pies. The bakery also offers a wide variety of ice cream and homemade milkshakes. Burris Farm Market has become a traditional stop and tourist attraction for countless people, families, and vacationers over the years.

7 days a week: 8:00 am to 6:00 pm

Strawberry Shortcake

4 cups chopped strawberries
4 cups sugar, divided
3 sticks butter, softened
6 eggs
4½ cups self-rising flour
1½ cups milk
1½ teaspoons vanilla extract
Whipping cream, whipped

Cover strawberries with 1 cup sugar or to taste; set aside 30 minutes for berries to make their own juice. Cream butter and 3 cups sugar. Add eggs and mix well. Add flour, milk and vanilla; beat 2 minutes. Pour into a treated 12x17-inch cake pan. Bake at 350° for 30 minutes. Divide into serving pieces and top with strawberries and whipped cream.

Restaurant Recipes

Sweet Strawberry Bread

2 cups all-purpose flour

2 cups sugar

1 teaspoon baking soda

1 teaspoon salt

1 teaspoon cinnamon

4 eggs beaten

1¼ cups vegetable oil

1 cup chopped pecans

2½ cups chopped strawberries

Combine first 5 ingredients and mix. Combine remaining 4 ingredients and add to dry mixture, stirring well. Spoon into 2 greased and floured loaf pans. Bake at 350° for 1 hour.

To make blueberry, peach, apple, banana, or zucchini, substitute equal amount of fruit.

Restaurant Recipe

Tomato Pie

¼ cup fresh basil

¼ sweet yellow onion, chopped

2 tablespoons olive oil

Salt and pepper to taste

2 cups chopped tomatoes

1 (9-inch) pre-baked pie crust

½ cup equal parts Cheddar and mozzarella cheese

2 tablespoons mayonnaise

In food processor, combine basil, onion, oil, salt and pepper. Process until creamy. Combine with tomatoes and pour in pie crust. Combine cheese and mayonnaise and spread over pie. Bake at 250° until golden brown, about 30 minutes.

Restaurant Recipe

THINKSTOCK/ISTOCK/OLDDAYS

The Brick Pit

5456 Old Shell Road
Mobile, AL 36608
251-343-0001 • www.brickpit.com

Ready for serious BBQ? Visit The Brick Pit. With meat that is smoked up to 30 hours, they are the Holy Grail of BBQ. You'll love their pulled pork and ribs that are thick and tender and their delicious sides. Don't miss Mrs. Waits Homemade Banana Pudding made from scratch every day. Eat in or take it home, either way, you will be impressed with their friendly staff, great food, and down-home kid-friendly atmosphere. Watch for them on the Travel Channel's show **Man vs. Food**, *101 Tastiest Places to Chow Down in America*, *Chow Down Countdown*, and *The 10 Best BBQ Joints in the US*.

Tuesday – Thursday: 11:00 am to 8:00 pm
Friday & Saturday: 11:00 am to 9 :00 pm

The Brick Pit
Bar B Que Baked Beans

1 (3-pound) can pork and beans

1 large onion, chopped

1 large bell pepper, diced

1½ cups BBQ sauce
(Brick Pit sauce if you can get it)

¼ pound smoked pulled pork, chopped
(or 7 slices bacon, cut in 1-inch pieces)

½ cup dark brown sugar

Preheat oven to 350°. Mix together first 5 ingredients and top with dark brown sugar. Place in 4-quart casserole dish and bake 45 minutes to 1 hour.

Restaurant Recipe

Butch Cassidy's Café Fried Green Tomatoes

Fresh green tomatoes

2 cups yellow corn flour

1 cup white cornmeal

2 tablespoons Tony Chachere's Creole seasoning

Buttermilk

Cut green tomatoes into ¼- to ⅜-inch slices (cut slices in half if preferred).

For batter mix, combine yellow corn flour, white cornmeal and Tony Chachere's.

Dip green tomato slices into bowl of buttermilk, then dip into batter mix generously covering. Fry until golden brown.

Serve with ranch dressing.

Restaurant Recipe

Butch Cassidy's Café

60 North Florida Street
Mobile, AL 36607
251-450-0690
www.butchcassidys.com

Butch Cassidy's Café is the perfect spot for pleasant dining and superb cuisine. Restaurant critics, first time visitors, and neighborhood regulars agree—the atmosphere is great, the food is superb, and the service is outstanding. The restaurant offers a casual atmosphere perfect for dining with friends, co-workers, and family members. The creative menu features a wide array of great selections, always made from the highest quality ingredients. Ask about the daily specials and other notable menu selections. The staff at Butch Cassidy's Café are friendly and professional and will ensure that your dining experience is a pleasant one.

Monday – Saturday: 11:00 am to 10:00 pm
Sunday: 11:00 am to 9:00 pm

Mary's Southern Cooking

"Where great cooking is just the beginning."

**3011 Springhill Avenue
Mobile, AL 36607
251-476-2232**

Mary's Southern Cooking is your place to enjoy the foods your grandmother cooked. Offering more than just down-home southern soul food, they specialize in gourmet food and are catering specialists. They do weddings, family events, picnics, and corporate events. No event is too big or too small for Mary's to handle. Stop by, meet Ms. Mary, enjoy the music, and get the best food cooked with the love of a grandma.

**Sunday – Friday: 11:00 am to 6:00 pm
Saturday: 11:00 am to 5:00 pm**

Fruit Bowl Cake

3 (3.4-ounce) packages instant banana pudding mix, plus ingredients to prepare per directions

1 (18x24-inch) sheet cake, prepared (4 prepared cake mixes)

2 (16-ounce) cartons Cool Whip

2 (21-ounce) cans blueberry pie filling

2 (21-ounce) cans strawberry pie filling

5 bananas, peeled and sliced

Fresh blueberries and strawberries for garnish, optional

In 3 separate bowls, prepare each box of pudding per directions; refrigerate (in separate bowls) until set. Cut sheet cake in 3 pieces. Place 1 piece in a pan. Layer 1 bowl banana pudding, 1 carton Cool Whip, 1 can blueberry pie filling, 1 can strawberry pie filling and half of the bananas over cake. Repeat all layers. Top with third piece of cake and third bowl of banana pudding. Garnish top with fresh blueberries and strawberries, if desired. Refrigerate until ready to serve. Feeds about 30 people.

Restaurant Recipe

Saucy Q Jambalaya

8 cups water (may need more)

1 stick butter

2 pounds boneless chicken, cut up

1 cup each chopped onion, chopped celery and chopped green bell pepper

1 teaspoon each salt, crushed red pepper, cayenne pepper and poultry seasoning

1½ teaspoons each thyme, garlic powder and black pepper

3 bay leaves

1 cup rice

1 pound sausage

1 cup pimentos

2 cups crushed tomatoes

2 cups diced tomatoes

2 cups ketchup

1 cup Saucy Q Sauce or your favorite barbecue sauce

Add water and butter to a large stockpot over medium-high heat. Add chicken, onion, celery, bell pepper and spices. Bring to a boil and boil 15 minutes; add rice. Boil an additional 10 minutes then reduce heat to low. Add remaining ingredients. Add more water for desired consistency; cook another 15 minutes. Stir occasionally. Serve hot with crackers.

Restaurant Recipe

Saucy Q BBQ

**1111 Government Street
Mobile, AL 36604
251-433-7427
www.saucyqbbq.com**

Saucy Q is owned by barbecue aficionado and Alabama native Elbert Wingfield, who says his family—Jacquelyn, Jarret, and Darnell—had three things in mind when starting the business: good service, a good attitude, and good food. Since starting the business in 1990, they have served the best barbecue in Alabama including the best ribs you'll ever eat plus beef and chicken that falls off the bone. Saucy Q's recipe is SMOKE, FIRE, and LOVE. They say, "Most of all we love what we are doing; to see the expression of joy and pleasure on our customers' faces, there's nothing like it."

**Monday – Wednesday:
10:00 am to 7:00 pm
Thursday – Saturday: 10:00 am to 9:00 pm
Sunday: Noon to 6:00 pm**

Spot of Tea

310 Dauphin Street
Mobile, AL 36602
251-433-9009
www.spotoftea.com

Spot of Tea has been "the place to be" in downtown Mobile for 20 years. Easily recognizable for its beautifully manicured side-walk café and modern Victorian dining room complete with piano on the main floor, they provide a unique dining experience for locals and guests alike. Serving the finest breakfast, sandwiches, seafood, steaks, soup, and special dishes in the area, Spot of Tea's food offers comfort and class, their clubs offer distinct aesthetics and variety, and the staff provides you with an experience that will exceed your expectations.

7 days a week: 7:00 am to 2:00 pm

TEACUP: THINKSTOCK/ISTOCK/MERIH UNAL OZMEN

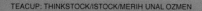

Eggs Cathedral

½ grilled English muffin

Crab cake of your choice

2 scrambled eggs

Seafood Bisque

Deadly Hash

Place English muffin in center of plate. Stack on the crab cake then eggs, stacking them high. Smother with Seafood Bisque. Arrange Deadly Hash around edge of plate.

Seafood Bisque:

½ cup butter or margarine

¾ cup flour, divided

2 cups heavy cream

¼ cup chicken or vegetable stock

1 tablespoon parsley flakes

6 ounces grouper chunks, deboned

4 ounces crawfish tail meat

Salt, pepper, garlic powder and seafood seasoning to taste

Melt butter in a saucepan. Slowly add ½ cup flour, whisking constantly. Once smooth, add heavy cream and stock. Simmer slowly over medium heat about 5 minutes. Add parsley, grouper and crawfish; simmer another 20 minutes until thickened. Add seasonings to taste.

Deadly Hash:

Square-cut potatoes to taste

Chopped bell pepper to taste

Chopped onion to taste

Pepperoncini to taste

Sauerkraut to taste

Shredded Cheddar cheese to taste

Fry enough potatoes for one serving in hot oil. Just before brown, add bell pepper, onion and pepperoncini. Cook until potatoes are brown; drain. Combine potato mixture with sauerkraut and cheese.

Restaurant Recipe

Fried Green Tomatoes

4 large green tomatoes

3 cups cornmeal

1 tablespoon salt or to taste

1 tablespoon pepper or to taste

Oil for frying

2 cups buttermilk

Wash and slice tomatoes approximately ⅜-inch thick. Season cornmeal with salt and pepper. Heat oil in skillet to 350°. Dip tomatoes in buttermilk, and then dip in seasoned cornmeal. Fry till golden brown. Drain on paper towels.

Restaurant Recipe

Whistle Stop

110 South Florida Street
Mobile, AL 36606

Since 1998, Mobile's Whistle Stop has been family owned and operated and located in the heart of midtown Mobile. With a railroad-themed décor and friendly atmosphere, you'll enjoy casual family dining at its best for breakfast, lunch, and dinner. From the time you walk in the door until the time you check out, you will be treated as family. Their promise is that everyone leaves happy—especially after one of the delicious homemade desserts. Sunday Brunch is always a hit! When you're in the area, stop by, eat, and have a cocktail with the friendly folks at Whistle Stop. You'll be glad you did!

**Tuesday & Wednesday:
7:00 am to 3:00 pm
Thursday – Saturday: 7:00 am to 9:00 pm
Sunday: 8:00 am to 3:00 pm**

Southern Coleslaw

5 pounds green cabbage, shredded

½ cup shredded purple cabbage

½ cup shredded carrots

1½ cups mayonnaise

¼ cup dill relish

2 teaspoons salt

1 tablespoon black pepper

1 teaspoon cayenne pepper, optional

Mix cabbages and carrots. In a separate bowl, combine mayonnaise, relish, salt and black pepper. Mix until sugar starts to melt. Add cayenne pepper, if desired, and then add to cabbage mixture. Chill 1 hour and serve. Makes 25 servings.

Restaurant Recipe

Southern Fried Soft Shell Crabs

2 soft shell crabs, fresh (preferred) or frozen

2 cups cornmeal

Seasoned salt to taste

Black pepper to taste

1 egg, beaten

½ cup milk

⅓ cup cold water

1 cup flour

Butter or oil for frying

Peel back, or pull back off of soft shells, and rinse center, cleaning well removing the fat. Make breading by combining cornmeal, seasoned salt and black pepper. Make milk wash by combining egg, milk and water. Dredge soft shells in flour, then dip in milk wash, then coat with seasoned cornmeal. Pan- or deep-fry until golden brown and crispy. Drain on paper towels. Eat them as-is or use for a sandwich or po' boy with mayonnaise, lettuce and tomato.

Restaurant Recipe

Whistle Stop Bread Pudding with Rum Sauce

1 loaf French bread, torn into chunks

1 quart (4 cups) milk

2 cups sugar

2 teaspoons vanilla extract

3 eggs

1 cup peeled and diced apples

½ cup raisins (soaked in rum)

3 tablespoons melted butter

Soak bread in milk for 30 minutes. Mix sugar, vanilla, eggs, apples and raisins. Add to bread and mix well. Put melted butter in 9x13-inch pan. Pour in bread mixture. Bake at 350° for 30 to 35 minutes, or until bubbly and hot.

Rum or Whiskey Sauce:

½ cup butter

1 cup sugar

1 teaspoon real vanilla extract

1 egg, beaten

About 6 to 8 ounces rum or whiskey

In a small saucepan, cream butter and sugar. Add vanilla. Slowly stir in egg then add rum. Cook over low heat, stirring, about 5 minutes. Serve warm over individual servings.

Makes 8 to 10 servings.

Restaurant Recipe

Mary's Macaroni and Cheese

2 cups elbow macaroni

1 teaspoon salt

½ stick butter

Pepper to taste

3 eggs

1 cup half-and-half

1 (2-cup) package shredded extra sharp Cheddar cheese

Bring about 6 cups water to a boil. Add macaroni and salt. Boil until macaroni is al dente; drain. Stir in butter. In a 9x9-inch pan, layer half the macaroni. Sprinkle with pepper. Top with a third of the cheese. Top with remaining macaroni, sprinkle with pepper. Beat eggs and cream; pour over macaroni. Top with remaining cheese. Bake at 400° for 30 minutes.

Restaurant Recipe

Mel's Dairy Dream

216 South Alabama Avenue
Monroeville, AL 36460
251-743-2483

Visit Mel's Dairy Dream and step back to a time when the pace of life was slower, the days were longer, and service was still a restaurant's top priority. You'll instantly know you are not at an average restaurant when drive up to Mel's building which was built in 1954. Enjoy outstanding hamburgers and milkshakes ordered the old-fashioned way by stepping up to the window and letting them know what you want. The food—from chicken and French fries to salads to gizzard and liver dinners—is always fresh. The steak sandwich is a local favorite.

Monday – Saturday: 10:00 am to 5:00 pm

INTERESTING FACT:

Next door to Mel's is the marker that commemorates the place where Truman Capote grew up as a child.

OLD COURTHOUSE MUSEUM

Monroeville, Alabama

Monroeville's two most famous citizens—Harper Lee and Truman Capote—are celebrated in permanent exhibits within Old Courthouse Museum. The courtroom, restored to its 1930's appearance, was the model for Harper Lee's fictional courtroom settings in her book, *To Kill a Mockingbird*. For the movie, the courtroom was completely recreated on a Hollywood sound stage. Today, fans of the classic novel and movie come to the courthouse from all over the world. Visitors are free to move throughout the courtroom, including the balcony, witness chair, judge's bench, and tables used by the prosecutor and defense attorney. Throughout her childhood, Harper Lee often sat in the balcony as she watched her father practice law in this very room.

TRUMAN CAPOTE
(1924 - 1984)

On this site stood the home of the Faulk family of Monroeville, relatives of the writer Truman Capote. Capote himself lived in this home between 1927 and c. 1933, and for several years spent his summer vacations here. Two of the Faulk sisters operated a highly successful millinery shop located on the town square. The third sister, affectionately known as "Sook," was the inspiration for characters in *The Grass Harp, The Thanksgiving Visitor,* and *A Christmas Memory.* The original structure on this site burned to the ground in 1940, and the second home was demolished in 1988. Monroeville remained important to Capote throughout his life, and he returned to the area many times in the years before his death to visit surviving relatives.

"I won't be here forever, Buddy. Nor will you....The Lord willing, you'll be here long after I've gone. And as long as you remember me, then we'll always be together."
-Truman Capote, *The Thanksgiving Visitor*
©1967, Random House, Inc.

ALABAMA HISTORICAL ASSOCIATION   1988

Radley's Fountain Grille

**1559 South Alabama Avenue
Monroeville, AL 36601
251-743-2348**

Radley's Fountain Grille, a mecca for thousands of visitors from all over the United States who attend the play adapted from Harper Lee's immortal novel "To Kill a Mockingbird," offers an extensive menu of hand-cut steaks, fresh Alabama seafood, and homemade soups and desserts, all served in a delightful atmosphere with superb service. The dining rooms are a unique blend of cherished family antiques, photographs, postcards and other items more than 100 years old. Signature foods are chicken salad, seafood gumbo, and a "BLT Supreme," selected as one of the "100 Dishes to Eat in Alabama Before You Die."

Monday – Saturday: 11:00 am to 8:00 pm

Potato Salad

1 gallon cooked diced potatoes

1 cup chopped celery

1 cup chopped sweet pickles

12 boiled eggs, diced

2 tablespoon Durkee's salad dressing

1 to 2 cups mayonnaise

1 tablespoon Tony Chachere's Creole seasoning or to taste

Salt and pepper to taste

Mix it up. Taste it. Adjust seasonings if needed. Refrigerate.

Restaurant Recipe

Creamy Chicken and Broccoli Soup

Served on Wednesdays at Radley's.

7½ cups sliced fresh mushrooms

7½ cups chopped onion

3½ cups butter or margarine, melted

3½ cups all-purpose flour

7½ quarts half-and-half or milk

5¾ quarts chicken broth

15 cups diced cooked fresh chicken

15 cups chopped broccoli, thawed or broccoli tops

1½ tablespoons dried whole rosemary

2½ tablespoons salt

1 tablespoon whole dried thyme

1 tablespoon pepper

Sauté mushrooms and onions in butter over low heat until tender. Add flour, stirring until smooth; cook 1 minute, stirring constantly. Gradually add half-and-half and chicken broth; cook over medium-low heat, stirring constantly until mixture is thickened and bubbly. Stir in diced chicken and remaining ingredients. Cover and simmer 10 minutes, stirring occasionally. To Store: Refrigerate in a tightly covered container up to 2 days or in the freezer up to 1 month. Serves 40.

Restaurant Recipe

Stuffed Celery

1 (3-ounce) package cream cheese, softened

1 tablespoon finely chopped pecans

1 tablespoon pineapple preserves or to taste

Mix well and stuff celery with it.

Family Favorite

Cosmo's Restaurant & Bar

25753 Canal Road
Orange Beach, AL 36561
251-948-WOOF (9663)

Off the beaten path, Cosmo's Restaurant & Bar is far from ordinary, serving fresh and eclectic food enticing even the most discriminate diner. From hand-cut steaks and local seafood to pastas and sushi, this neighborhood favorite takes cuisine to the cutting edge. Culinary greats like chicken roulade wrapped in bacon, sesame seared tuna salad, and traditional crab cakes with a twist will have you wanting more. The Year of Alabama Food named their Banana Leaf Wrapped Fish as one of the top "100 Dishes to Eat in Alabama Before You Die." This epicurean delight is just one of the many masterpieces created daily in this out-of-the-way hot spot.

Sunday – Thursday: 11:00 am to 9:30 pm
Friday & Saturday: 11:00 am to 10:00 pm

Nutter Butter Banana Pudding

1 (5.1-ounce) box instant vanilla pudding plus ingredients to prepare per directions

2 teaspoons vanilla extract

1 (16-ounce) carton Cool Whip

5 medium-size ripe bananas, sliced to ¼ inch

1 (1-pound) package Nutter Butter cookies, broken into thirds

Prepare pudding per package directions. Add vanilla to half the Cool Whip then stir into pudding. Spoon a third of pudding into a 3-quart glass serving bowl or trifle dish. Top with half of bananas and cookies. Repeat layers ending with remaining pudding. Top with remaining Cool Whip. Refrigerate at least 2 hours before serving.

Local Favorite

Divinity

4 egg whites

4 cups sugar

½ cup white corn syrup

1 cup water

¼ teaspoon salt

1 teaspoon vanilla extract

Pecan halves

Beat egg whites until stiff. Cook sugar, syrup, water, salt and vanilla to 240° (soft ball stage). Pour ½ cup over beaten egg whites, beating constantly. Continue cooking syrup to 260° (hard ball stage). Pour slowly over egg white mixture and continue beating until divinity holds peaks. Spoon onto greased waxed paper, and place a pecan half on each piece.

Restaurant Recipe

Punta Clara Kitchen

**17111 Scenic Highway 98
Point Clear, AL 36564
251-928-8477 • www.puntaclara.com**

What began in 1952 as a backyard hobby by Dorothy Brodbeck Pacey, has flourished and grown into Punta Clara Kitchen, a family-owned and operated business that now involves four generations of Paceys. The candy kitchen resides in our turn-of-the-century Victorian family home in Point Clear. Our specialty candies are still made "from scratch" using old, treasured family recipes. We think you'll agree that they are the best you've ever tasted.

**Monday – Saturday: 9:00 am to 5:00 pm
Sunday: 12:30 pm to 5:00 pm**

The Wash House Restaurant

17111 Scenic Highway 98
Point Clear, AL 36532
251-928-4838
www.washhouserestaurant.com

The Wash House Restaurant serves up fine southern coastal cuisine in a casual atmosphere with a generous helping of southern hospitality. The menu features a delicious selection of steak, seafood, and a lot more—all freshly prepared using the best ingredients available. Local favorites include the Shrimp Stack appetizer, Châteaubriand, and their specialty drinks. Don't miss the Key Lime Bread Pudding—exquisite. The ambience is rustic but elegant, cozy and romantic. Semi-casual attire is accepted and reservations are recommended. An area is available for private parties of any size; catering is available for occasions big and small.

7 days a week: 5:00 pm to 9:30 pm
Reservations recommended

Key Lime Bread Pudding

Topping:

½ cup sugar

1 cup graham cracker crumbs

¼ pound (1 stick) butter, melted

Mix sugar and cracker crumbs in bowl. Add melted butter. Stir until thoroughly mixed. Set aside.

Bread Pudding:

5 (4-inch) stale yeast rolls

10 to 12 eggs

1 pint half-and-half

1 cup powdered sugar

1 teaspoon vanilla extract

Cut stale rolls in half length-wise (into tops and bottoms). Mix eggs, half-and-half, powdered sugar and vanilla thoroughly. Add bread and soak until saturated. Place bread onto greased sheet pan. Bake at 425° for 6 to 10 minutes, until lightly brown. Immediately loosen bread from pan to prevent sticking.

Filling:

12 egg yolks

3 (14-ounce) cans sweetened condensed milk

¾ cup Key lime juice

Mix egg yolks and milk thoroughly in bowl. Line a 9x9-inch greased sheet pan with cooked bread. Slowly stir Key lime juice into egg mixture mixing well. Pour over bread. Top with graham cracker mixture. Bake at 375 ° for 12 minutes. Chill before serving.

Restaurant Recipe

The Bake Shoppe Café

The Sweeter Things in Life

22245 Highway 59, Suite 4B
Robertsdale, AL 36567
251-947-4701
www.thebakeshoppecafe.com
www.facebook.com/TheBakeShoppeCafe

The Bake Shoppe Café is a full-service restaurant offering a full lunch menu with daily specials and desserts and includes a custom bakery. Food is made to order so you enjoy fresh dishes each time you order. At the bakery, everything is made special for the customer so a 48-hour notice is required on bakery orders. Seasoning blends, sauces, soups, and baked goods are homemade by Juan. A local favorite is the fish tacos which are served daily and have been featured on local television three times and in three food showcases.

Monday – Friday: 10:00 am to 5:00 pm
Saturday: 10:00 am to 2:00 pm

Fish Tacos

Juan's Tangy Mayo:

½ cup mayonnaise

½ cup ketchup

½ cup hot sauce (we use Franks)

1 tablespoon salt and pepper

Mix all ingredients in a bowl and chill until ready to use.

Corn & Black Bean Salsa:

1 (15½-ounce) can whole-kernel corn, drained

1 (14-ounce) can black beans, drained

½ onion, small diced

½ green bell pepper, small diced

1 tomato, diced

Salt and pepper

1 tablespoon white vinegar

Mix all ingredients in a bowl and set aside.

Fish Tacos:

4 (6-ounce) portions white flaky fish (we use tilapia)

Salt, pepper, Creole seasoning, or your preferred seasoning for fish

2 soft flour tortillas

Shredded lettuce

Shredded cheese

Corn & Black Bean Salsa

Juan's Tangy Mayo

Season fish to taste and grill 2 to 3 minutes per side, or until fully cooked. Warm tortillas. Cut fish in half and place pieces on tortillas. Top fish with shredded lettuce, cheese and Corn & Black Bean Salsa. Drizzle with Juan's Tangy Mayo.

Restaurant Recipe

Right On I-10 But Far Off The Beaten Track!

Located Inside

Exit 53, I-10 West
27801 County Road 64
Robertsdale, AL 36567
251-960-1152

The Derailed Diner is a travel-themed restaurant serving made-from-scratch great American food in the most unique setting this side of the Orient Express. Our full size 1920's era train dining car, real truck bed tables and yellow school bus lunch counter are jaw dropping backdrops for our award winning dishes. Chef Rick's Pecan Pie Cheesecake is featured in Alabama Tourism's "100 Dishes To Eat In Alabama Before You Die." Be sure to try our popular Derailed Diner Hobo Basket, too. A feast of meat and fresh vegetables slow roasted in foil, and absolutely no hobos were harmed in the making of this dish!

Open 24/7
Closed Mondays 10:00 pm to 6:00 am

Subway and Chester's Chicken also available for hungry travelers who need a meal to go.

Derailed Diner's Sweet Corn Bread

(the most requested recipe from our facebook fans)

1 cup yellow cornmeal
1 cup self-rising flour
1 cup sugar
2 eggs
1¾ cups whole milk
¼ pound (1 stick) butter

Combine dry ingredients. In a separate bowl, beat eggs and milk together; slowly add melted butter. Mix into dry ingredients until smooth. Pour into a greased 10x10-inch baking dish and bake 25 minutes at 400°. Cook on rack before cutting.

Chocolate Cobbler

Brownie:

6 tablespoon butter, melted

1 cup self-rising flour

¾ cup sugar

2 tablespoons cocoa

½ cup whole milk

1 teaspoon vanilla extract

Mix above ingredients (batter will be stiff). Pour into greased (or use nonstick spray) 9x13-inch pan.

Topping:

1 cup sugar

¼ cup cocoa

1½ cups boiling water

Combine dry ingredients and sprinkle over brownie batter. Pour boiling water evenly over entire mixture; do not stir. Bake 30 minutes. (Do not over bake.) Serve warm with vanilla bean ice cream. Yum Yum!

Restaurant Recipe

Magnolia Blossom Café

**22667 Highway 59 South
Robertsdale, AL 36567
251-947-0081**

After traveling the country and abroad for many years, raising a family, and retiring from construction, Darlene and Charles Roper purchased The Magnolia Blossom Café—a combination of buffet and menu dining offering steak and seafood all day, six days a week along with a country lunch buffet seven days. Evenings are menu-only except Friday night which offers a Seafood and Prime Rib Buffet. The Blossom has always strived for a country, casual dining experience with good wholesome country food like you would get at "grandma's" house. The signature Eggplant Sandwich is a local favorite.

**Sunday – Wednesday: 7:00 am to 2:30 pm
Thursday – Saturday: 7:00 am to 8:30 pm**

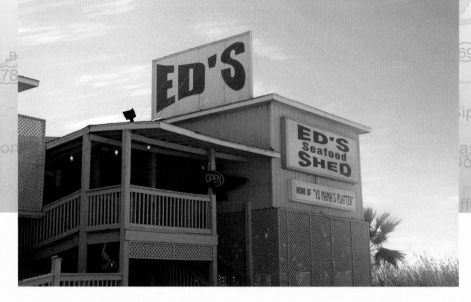

Ed's Seafood Shed

Home of "Yo Mama's Platter"

3382 Battleship Parkway • Spanish Fort, AL 36527
251-625-1947 • www.edsshed.com
www.facebook.com/eds.seafoodshed/timeline

Ed's Seafood Shed, family owned and operated, is located on Battleship Parkway so you can enjoy the best sunset on Mobile Bay on their spacious deck. The signature "Yo Mama's Platter" is served family-style beginning with Ed's famous coleslaw, garlic cheese grits, turnip greens, and gumbo. Next comes a generous platter of fried shrimp, scallops, oysters, crab claws, and fish along with French fries and hushpuppies. If that's not enough, it's topped off with home-made devil's food cake with strawberry sauce, hot fudge, whipped cream, and pecans on top. As they say, "Join us at Ed's for seafood cooked THE OLD MOBILE WAY!"

Sunday – Thursday: 11:00 am to 9:00 pm
Friday & Saturday: 11:00 am to 11:00 pm

Grilled Triggerfish Bienville

2 (8-ounce) triggerfish fillets

Creole seasoning

¼ cup diced Conecuh sausage

¼ cup diced onion

⅛ cup diced green pepper

⅛ cup diced red pepper

¼ cup chopped fresh mushrooms

¼ cup white wine

¾ cup half-and-half

4 ounces peeled and deveined crawfish tails (shrimp are great also)

Salt and pepper to taste

Chopped green onions for garnish

Season fish fillets with Creole seasoning to taste; set aside. Sauté sausage until browned; remove sausage, reserving oil in pan. Sauté onion, peppers and mushrooms over medium heat in reserved oil until just cooked through. Add sausage back to pan and cook 2 minutes more; remove mixture. Deglaze pan with white wine, add sausage mixture back to pan, and reduce heat to low. Add half-and-half, crawfish tails, and salt and pepper to taste; simmer until fish is ready. Heat grill pan to medium-high. Cook fish fillets, skin side down, 3 minutes. Carefully turn fish and finish cooking, approximately 2 more minutes. Plate fish on your favorite platter and carefully top with sauce. Garnish edge of plate with Creole seasoning and all over with green onions. Enjoy!

Restaurant Recipe

ED'S SEAFOOD SHED

HOME of YO MAMA'S PLATTER

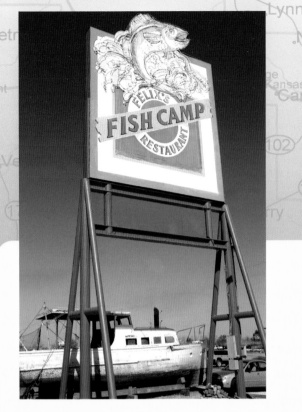

Felix's Fish Camp Restaurant

1530 Battleship Parkway
Spanish Fort, AL 36527
251-626-6710
www.felixsfishcamp.com

Felix's Fish Camp, located on scenic Mobile Bay Causeway, features fresh seafood and USDA certified steaks. You'll enjoy entrées prepared from classic Mobile recipes plus a few new ones. The food is just the beginning, at Felix's you enjoy the best service in the Southeast because they make guests the most important people in town. And if that's not

enough, Felix's Fish Camp is situated on one of the most scenic parts of Mobile Bay. From gigantic windows you can take in an entire panorama of natural beauty. Felix's offers a terrific venue for business meetings, birthday parties, graduation dinners, wedding rehearsals or family reunions.

Monday – Sunday:
11:00 am to 10:00 pm

Felix's Crab-Stuffed Shrimp Scampi with White Wine Garlic Butter

White Wine Garlic Butter:

1 cup melted butter or margarine

2 tablespoons fresh minced garlic

1 teaspoon dried leaf oregano

2 tablespoons fresh lemon juice

1 tablespoon white wine

Combine all ingredients. Makes 1¼ cups.

Note: Cover and refrigerate leftover garlic butter up to 1 week for later use.

Crabmeat Stuffing:

2½ cups fresh, soft, fine breadcrumbs, crusts included

1 egg, beaten

¾ cup mayonnaise

⅓ cup each: finely diced celery, green bell pepper and green onion

1 tablespoon Old Bay seasoning

1 tablespoon minced fresh parsley

1 tablespoon fresh lemon juice

1 teaspoon Worcestershire sauce

2 teaspoons yellow mustard

¼ teaspoon black pepper

Dash Tabasco

1 pound lump crabmeat (dark leg meat may be used)

Combine all stuffing ingredients, except crabmeat, in a bowl; mix well, by hand. Add crabmeat. Gently toss until evenly mixed.

Note: Wrap any remaining crabmeat stuffing and refrigerate up to 3 days or freeze for up to a month.

Crab-Stuffed Shrimp Scampi:

5 large (16-20 count or 21-25 count) shrimp per order, peeled, tail intact and butterflied

Old Bay seasoning

Chopped parsley

Preheat oven to 550°. Use convection oven if available. Layer 1 tablespoon Crabmeat Stuffing inside each shrimp, butterflied side down. Press shrimp tail on top of stuffing.

Spread 1 tablespoon White Wine Garlic Butter on bottom of 12-ounce rarebit or small casserole. Lay 5 stuffed shrimp on top of garlic butter. Sprinkle small amount Old Bay seasoning on stuffed shrimp. Spread 1 additional tablespoon garlic butter over the 5 shrimp. Bake, uncovered, 5 to 6 minutes. Remove from oven; sprinkle shrimp with chopped parsley.

Serve with lemon wedge and crusty bread.

Restaurant Recipe

Stagecoach Café

52860 State Highway 59
Stockton, AL 36579
251-580-0608

Located in historic Stockton, Stagecoach Café beckons you to step back to a time when life moved at a much slower pace. Enjoy the daily buffet of home-style meats and vegetable or order from the menu—fresh, never frozen seafood, mouth-watering 8- or 14-ounce rib-eyes cooked just the way you like, and much more. After a delicious meal, relax in the rocking chairs on the front porch. Stagecoach Café offers a guarantee— "We guarantee that only your mother's cooking could equal what you'll find at Stagecoach Café."

Monday – Wednesday:
10:30 am to 9:00 pm
Thursday & Friday: 10:30 am to 9:00 pm
Saturday: 7:00 am to 10:00 pm
Sunday: 10:30 am to 3:00 pm

Buttermilk Pie

Crust:

3 cups graham cracker crumbs

1 cup sugar

1½ sticks butter, melted

Combine ingredients and press half into each of 2 (9x13-inch) pans.

Pie:

5 cups sugar

1¼ cups self-rising flour

2 cups buttermilk

1½ cups melted butter

10 eggs, beaten

1 tablespoon vanilla extract

1 cup coconut, optional

Mix ingredients in order listed. Divide between the 2 crusts. Bake at 350° about 45 minutes or until set. (For Chocolate Buttermilk Pie, add 1 cup cocoa.)

Restaurant Recipe

Roast Beef

1 (about 18-pound) full beef roast

2 tablespoons Greek seasoning

1 tablespoon Italian seasoning

1 tablespoon garlic powder

3 tablespoons mustard

1 teaspoon Lawry's seasoned salt

8 cups au jus (beef juice)

Unwrap roast and lay, fat side down, in a deep, full-sized hotel pan. Sprinkle about half of the spices over roast and use your hands to massage the spices over the meat. Turn roast over (fat side up) and sprinkle remaining spices over roast. Again, use your hands to massage spices fully into the meat. Pour au jus (prepared per package directions) into bottom of pan. Cover pan with foil, making sure it seals the pan well.

Small: the roast does not touch the sides of the pan. Bake 12 hours at 250°.

Medium: the roast touches on at least two sides of the pan. Bake 12 hours at 260°.

Large: the roast is squeezed against all sides of the pan. Bake 12 hours at 265°.

Restaurant Recipe

Time to Eat Café

7351 Theodore-Dawes Road
Theodore, AL 36582
251-654-0228
www.timetoeatmobile.com

In 2000, a son decided to open a restaurant for his mother, who, as a single mom raised four kids by working in restaurants. In her 30+ years of working in restaurants in the Mobile area, she learned exactly the level of charm and hospitality southerners desire in restaurant service, as well as the large portions of tasty comfort food for which the South is known. So, for a true taste of southern food and hospitality, drop in to Time to Eat, Mobile's BEST Country Cookin'.

Monday – Saturday: 7:00 am to 9:00 pm
Sunday: 7:00 am to 3:00 pm

BELLINGRATH GARDENS
Theodore, Alabama

Bellingrath Gardens and Home was created by Mr. and Mrs. Walter Bellingrath and was first opened to the public in 1932. The property was originally purchased by Mr. Bellingrath in 1917 as a fishing camp. Mrs. Bellingrath began developing the gardens with architect George Bigelow Rogers in 1927. The home, completed in 1935, encompasses 10,500 square feet and features hand-made bricks salvaged from the 1852 birthplace of Alva Smith Vanderbilt Belmont in Mobile. Ironwork was obtained from the demolished circa 1837 Southern Hotel, also in Mobile. Throughout the year, this 65-acre Garden Estate is in full bloom with camellias in winter, azaleas in spring, roses in summer, chrysanthemums in autumn and Magic Christmas in Lights during the holiday season.

For more information, visit www.bellingrath.org

ISTOCK/COBRAPHOTO

Jean's Bread Pudding

6 eggs, beaten

2¼ cups milk

2 cup sugar

2 teaspoons vanilla extract

18 slices bread

Topping:

2¼ cups powdered sugar

⅓ cup milk

Combine eggs, milk, sugar and vanilla in a large bowl. Break bread into small pieces and add to mixture. Stir with a spoon to mix well ensuring that all the bread is well soaked. Spoon in a treated 9x13-inch pan. Bake at 375° for 45 minutes. (Baking time may vary depending on your oven; remove from oven when pudding is set.) Combine topping ingredients and spoon over bread pudding while warm. Let stand 45 minutes before slicing.

Restaurant Recipe

Gaston's Grill

33801 Highway 43
Thomasville, AL 36784
334-636-5444

Gaston's Grill is a family restaurant serving home cooked meals and the best burgers and steaks around. Lunch and dinner offer a hot bar featuring down-home meats and vegetables just like Grandma cooked. Breakfast is served every day from the menu featuring delicious, made-from-scratch options. A breakfast buffet is offered Saturday and Sunday mornings. Throughout the day a wide selection of sandwiches, hamburger steaks, pork chops, chicken tenders, salads, hand-cut rib-eye steaks, and fresh Gulf seafood are freshly prepared. Gaston's homemade onion rings or home fries are always a favorite.

7 days a week: 5:00 am to 9:00 pm

People's Corner

4 West Front Street South
Thomasville, AL 36784
334-636-6922

For more than three years, the People's Corner has been serving delicious food and desserts in historic downtown Thomasville. The beautiful People's Corner building was built in 1905. Customers come in daily to a home-style cooked lunch special. The People's Corner is famous for homemade desserts, milkshakes, coke floats, and banana splits. Along with the daily special, the menu is loaded with sandwiches and salads. Catering is also available. They are open for breakfast and lunch. So come join the girls at The Corner, that's People's Corner, where the elite meet to eat in historic downtown Thomasville!

Monday – Friday: 7:00 am to 2:00 pm

Crustless Egg Custard Pie

4 eggs, beaten

1⅓ cups milk

4 tablespoons melted butter

1 teaspoon vanilla extract

½ cup flour

1¾ cups sugar

Mix wet ingredients. Add flour and sugar. Pour in greased pie pan and bake at 350° for 45 minutes.

Restaurant Recipe

Cheesy Chicken Chili

1 pound cooked chicken, shredded

2 (15-ounce) cans pinto beans

2 (15-ounce) cans chili beans

2 (15-ounce) cans kidney beans

2 (14.5-ounce) cans Rotel tomatoes

Chili powder, cayenne pepper and garlic powder to taste

1 pint whipping cream

2 cups shredded pepper jack cheese

1 (16-ounce) container sour cream

Combine chicken, beans, tomatoes and seasonings in a crockpot. Cook 7 hours on low. Then add whipping cream, cheese, and sour cream; cook 1 more hour.

Restaurant Recipe

Squash Dressing

2 cups sliced yellow squash

1 large onion, chopped

2 cups crumbled cornbread

½ cup margarine, melted

1 cup shredded mild Cheddar cheese

¼ teaspoon Tony Chachere's
Creole seasoning

1 (10.75-ounce) can cream of
chicken soup

¼ cup milk

Pepper to taste

Place squash and onion in a pot, add water to cover and stew over medium heat until tender. Preheat oven to 350°. Lightly grease a 3-quart baking dish. Combine remaining ingredients in a large bowl. Drain squash and onion then add to cornbread mixture. Transfer to prepared baking dish. Bake 45 minutes, until lightly browned.

Restaurant Recipe

Chicken Salad

5 pounds boneless chicken breast

1 large red onion, chopped

1 bell pepper, chopped

5 boiled eggs, chopped

1½ to 2 cups mayonnaise

1½ cups pickle relish

1 tablespoon Tony Chachere's
Creole seasoning

Pepper to taste

Boil chicken until cooked all the way through. Shred. In a food processor, purée chopped onion, bell pepper and eggs. Mix together shredded chicken, puréed mixture and remaining ingredients.

Restaurant Recipe

Index of Restaurants

Index of Restaurants

Index of Recipes

Index of Recipes

C

Index of Recipes

Index of Recipes

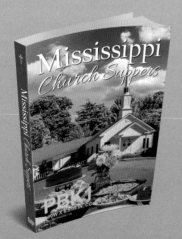

State Back Road Restaurants Series

From two-lane highways and interstates, to dirt roads and quaint downtowns, every road leads to delicious food when traveling across our United States. The STATE BACK ROAD RESTAURANTS COOKBOOK SERIES serves up a well-researched and charming guide to each state's best back road restaurants. No time to travel? No problem. Each restaurant shares with you their favorite recipes—sometimes their signature dish, sometimes a family favorite, but always delicious.

EACH: **$18.95** • **256 pages** • **7x9** • **paperbound** • **full-color**

Alabama
978-1-934817-13-1

Kentucky
978-1-934817-17-9

Tennessee
978-1-934817-21-6

Texas
978-1-934817-25-4

Don't miss out on our upcoming titles—join our Cookbook Club and you'll be notified of each new edition.

www.GreatAmericanPublishers.com • www.facebook.com/GreatAmericanPublishers

---

ORDER FORM

Mail to: Great American Publishers • 171 Lone Pine Church Road • Lena, MS 39094
Or call us toll-free 1.888.854.5954 to order by check or credit card.

❏ Check Enclosed

Charge to: ❏ Visa   ❏ MC   ❏ AmEx   ❏ Disc

Card#_____

Exp Date_____

Signature_____

Name_____

Address _____

City_____ State_____ Zip_____

Phone_____

Email_____

QTY.	TITLE	TOTAL
___	_____	____
___	_____	____
___	_____	____
___	_____	____
___	_____	____

Subtotal _____

Postage ($4 first book; $1 each additional) _____

Order 5 or more books, get FREE shipping

Total _____